OUT OF THE NIGHT

THE SPIRITUAL JOURNEY OF VIETNAM VETS

OUT OF THE NIGHT

THE SPIRITUAL JOURNEY OF VIETNAM VETS

WILLIAM P. MAHEDY

RADIX PRESS
-2004-

Out of the Night:
The Spiritual Journey of Vietnam Vets

Published by:

Radix Press
an imprint of Greyhound Books
5001 Chapman Highway
Knoxville, TN 37920
865-577-2229
radixpress.com

First published by Ballantine Books, a division of Random House, Inc., New York, NY, in 1986.

ISBN trade paperback 1-59677-003-1

This book is dedicated to Vietnam vets with profound respect and deep affection.

OUT OF THE NIGHT:
THE SPIRITUAL JOURNEY OF VIETNAM VETS
INTRODUCTION TO 2004 EDITION

The plane had landed at the Moscow airport. We were at last in the Soviet Union. The year was 1988 and I was with a team of 21 Americans, many of us Vietnam veterans and we had come at the invitation of a private Soviet foundation to work with Russian veterans of the war in Afghanistan. We did not know what would happen at the first face-to-face meeting with combat veterans of the two superpowers who had fought each other in Vietnam and in Afghanistan through surrogate forces. We knew the hated Soviets were our enemies and we they knew we had been theirs. As we passed through the customs and immigration gates, I felt chilled by the stares from the officials. I wondered at that moment whether going into the enemy's capital was really a good idea.

We were not all through the gates when we were confronted by young Russian men who had slipped through the gates. They spoke no English and had no translators with them. They asked if we were the "Americanetz Vietnamsy." We knew enough to translate: "American Vietnam veterans." The moment of truth had arrived. We identified ourselves and they immediately began to shower us with gifts of Russian medals and other tokens. They shook our hands and embraced us. When we finally got outside, we were greeted by more veterans and by translators, most of whom were young college students fluent in English and most of whom had never met an American nor been outside of Russia.

With a translator present and with a TV camera recording, Nicolai pointed to his prosthetic leg and said he had been wounded by an American-made machine gun. Jack, one of our team, responded that he had been wounded by a Russian-made rocket. They embraced and Nicolai said: "moi brot," "my brother." And so the die was cast. We were brothers because we had come from a great distance to help them. Both sides knew the personal cost of war and we were willing to help each other across the bridge of superpower enmity.

We spent the next night sitting around swapping stories of our wars and Russians and Americans who had lost limbs in combat took off their prosthetics and compared them. By the end of the first week, four of us Americans were sitting in a very large room in Moscow running a group therapy session for young Russian combat vets with Post Traumatic Stress (PTSD) while Russian psychiatrists and psychologists observed what we were doing.

Our work there showed us that PTSD is the same for veterans of both sides of every war. We found that the moral, spiritual and religious issues were largely the same for all of us. I had brought a few copies of the recently published *Out of the Night* and gave them to the Russians who could read English. Those who read the book later wrote me that they had benefited from it. I understood then that what I had written in that book had application far beyond our own culture and our own wars. The horrible residue of war is, tragically, universal.

One of the most enduring memories from my first Russian visit was our trip from our Moscow hotel to the depot to catch the midnight train to Leningrad. We were escorted by bus with Russian veterans and translators who had brought guitars and serenaded us with Russian songs. We also sang together American songs they could play and sing. Our attitudes towards the wars we had fought and our mutually hostile past was summed up best as we sang together; "We shall overcome." That song and that moment sum up my work with veterans and the spirit of this book. Together we can overcome the spiritual wounds of war.

Since *Out of the Night* was first published in 1986, it has been widely read by veterans, their families and by people interested in the spiritual, moral and religious issues of war. It has been used by therapists in VA clinics as a part of treatment programs for veterans dealing with combat stress.

During the years since the book first appeared, the country has begun to come to terms with the Vietnam War and with its veterans. The VA, having learned from the experience of the Vet Centers, has opened Post Traumatic Stress Disorder (PTSD) clinics in its medical centers. World War II and Korean War veterans have come in for treatment along with increasing numbers of Vietnam veterans and veterans of our more recent wars.

The Vet Center program has expanded and the VA has opened both inpatient and outpatient programs for veterans suffering from combat-related stress. Treatment for PTSD has greatly improved. Vietnam veterans have, in many ways, received at last a genuine "welcome home." There has been some public discussion of the religious and moral issues raised in the book.

Since the publication of the book I spent several more years working in a VA clinic where it was my privilege to treat not only Vietnam veterans, but those who saw combat in World War II, Korea and those who fought in our subsequent wars in the Persian Gulf, Somalia and the Balkans. A "spiritual recovery" program for combat veterans which I devised from the principles discussed in the book, showed me that *Out of the Night* is timeless

Now we are engaged in a major war in Iraq and the hunt for Al Qaeda in Afghanistan, creating another generation of new veterans. Vet Centers and VA clinics are already seeing an influx of these newest veterans—and this is only the first wave of those men and women already released from active duty.

Once again the country is divided over a war which seems to have no end in sight. Once again, troops are called upon to fight a war against an insurgency that seems to grow stronger. Once again the American military is called upon to chase an enemy into the midst of a civilian population. Once again the American military is seen by an indigenous population as oppressors. As was the case in Vietnam, the origins and conduct of the war seem grounded in erroneous intelligence, misjudgments, mistakes and outright deception on the part of political leaders.

Soldiers and their families are beginning to raise their voices in protest about shabby medical treatment they have received back home. Multiple deployments of military personnel back into the war zone have caused serious morale problems among the troops. Reserve and National Guard units have been called up and deployed in ways not seen since World War II.

Once again the American civil religion—which is often confused with authentic Christianity—has been used as a religious and moral underpinning for war. The discussion of civil religion in *Out of the Night* is as relevant today as when it was written. The religious rhetoric used to support the war in Iraq is even more blatant and virulent than that used during Vietnam. The dangerous doctrine of American exceptionalism which formed the basis for this pre-emptive war has its roots in civil religion. There has never been a greater need for a public conversation about religion and war than there is now. *Out of the Night* provides a framework for this discussion.

Discussions with counselors who work with newly returned

veterans of the wars in Afghanistan and Iraq and some personal contact with these veterans make it abundantly clear that the questions and problems confronting these young men and women are the same as those that plagued older generations of warriors. The sole exception and crucial difference between these new veterans and those who returned from Vietnam is that the country has learned from the bitter experience of a generation ago that we must provide support for our troops. We must not scapegoat them for whatever errors the civilian authorities might make in the decision to go to war and the blunders they make in fighting the war. As are other Vietnam vets, I am profoundly grateful for the support our troops have received during this war. I like to think that this book has played a small part in making Americans aware that veterans need our support, whatever we may think of the war itself.

Radix Press, believing as I do that *Out of the Night* is both timeless and timely, has responded to countless requests to republish the book. I am grateful to this publishing house and its president, Cyndy Mobley for making the book available again.

ACKNOWLEDGMENTS

This book could not have been written without the encouragement and loving support of my wife, Carol. Her careful editing of the manuscript and her suggestions greatly improved the book.

Michelle Rapkin, my editor at Ballantine Books for so many months, worked with me every step of the way, improving, editing, critiquing, and encouraging. I am deeply grateful to her. Ernest Tremblay's editing and Sandra Dijkstra's assistance have also contributed significantly to the book. I'm also grateful to Chris Carstens for his encouragement and advice. Walter Capps, my friend and Professor of Religious Studies at the University of California, Santa Barbara, insisted that I write this book. My participation in his classes and seminars and our work together in conducting training sessions for Vet Center counselors provided the intellectual stimulus required for writing.

The book grows out of an experience, an experience not only of war, but of healing the scars of war. Some of those men and women who put together the Vietnam veterans "movement" and the Vet Centers in particular are mentioned in the book, but many others are not. Their contributions are enormous, not only to this book—for it is, after all, only a book—but to their fellow vets and to the American people. I hope that the significance of what they have done will someday be recognized. In addition to those whose names are mentioned in the body of the book, I must acknowledge on this page some others whose selfless dedication remains an inspiration to me: Art Blank, Harold Bryant, Mike McWatters, Jack Smith, Dave Hill. Finally, and for me foremost among the healers, Pat Hoffmann, who looked after me in Vietnam.

INTRODUCTION

America is convinced by now that it knows its Vietnam veterans well. Not so long ago the nation watched them on its television screens as they went into combat in Southeast Asia. For the first time in the history of warfare an audience of people back home watched their soldiers die, heard them cry out in the agony of their wounds. A nation watched in fascination as its warrior sons went out on search-and-destroy missions among far-off peasant people.

When the vets returned from combat we listened to their strident voices as they opposed their own war. We watched them fling down their medals in anger and disgust. More recently we have listened to their personal stories and read their autobiographies. We have watched them welcomed home at last, honored by national salutes and parades. Finally, we have wept with them in the mystic presence of the memorial on the Washington Mall.

But do we really understand the vets? Have we ever recognized their moral anguish and grappled with what their pain means for all of us? Have the churches ever come to grips with the reason so many vets lost their religious faith during their time in Vietnam? I believe the answer to these questions is "no." America has not yet confronted the moral and religious questions for which the vets demand answers. Nor has a nation which prizes an upbeat optimistic mood yet recognized that many of its vets inhabit a world of spiritual bleakness—a "dark night of the soul." America still denies kinship with its sons and daughters in their pilgrimage through difficult spiritual terrain. But their journey is America's, their darkness is ours as well and so too is the path they have begun to travel in their journey out of the night.

This book attempts to probe the religious and moral issues which arose in Vietnam and which have not really been addressed in public. It also examines the loss of faith among the vets and traces the paths by which some have begun to rediscover belief in God. The book connects the vets' "dark night" experience with what Scripture and the Christian mystics have to say about similar states of soul. Finally, the book offers some suggestions which may be useful in plotting the course of one's own journey.

I know Vietnam veterans well, having taught some of them at both the high school and college levels before I entered the service myself and went overseas with them. I served three years as an Army chaplain with one tour in Vietnam. Upon discharge I was employed by the Veterans Administration in a social work capacity. During my years with the VA, I worked largely with Vietnam vets who had readjustment problems, and it was my great privilege to have had a small part in formulating the Vietnam Veterans Readjustment Counseling Program (the VA's "store" front Vet Centers). As the director of a Vet Center, I was associated with this program during its first years. Since leaving federal service I have been called upon often by individual veterans, by the VA, and by mental health professionals to act as a consultant regarding the moral and spiritual problems of those who fought the Vietnam War.

Though I have made extensive use of the biographical and clinical literature now available, most of the material from this book has been compiled in the course of my own ministry to soldiers in the field during my tour in Vietnam and my work with veterans after the war. The book is the result of my close personal involvement with hundreds of soldiers and veterans over a period of more than fifteen years. These men and women were searching for answers to the most serious questions any of us will ever confront. Their spiritual quest inspired me on my own journey and some of them have encouraged me to write this book.

Even though I am a veteran, I did not write my own story or that of the military chaplaincy. This book is a chronicle of the spiritual journey of young men and women (average age slightly more than nineteen years) who found themselves in a cauldron of violence which shattered their faith and called into questions their most basic values.

A word about the religious frame of reference, the prism through which my analysis of the vets' spiritual journey is refracted. The book is written from a Christian point of view for three reasons. First, Christian language is used in public discourse in the United States, often having an impact upon policy decisions. Second, most of the vets I encouraged had some connection with a Christian church. Third, I am a believing, practicing Christian. For eighteen years I was a member of a Roman Catholic religious community (the Augustinians), and I served as a Roman Catholic chaplain in Vietnam. For the past ten years I have been a priest in the Episcopal Church.

This book is intended for a wider readership than Vietnam veterans. One of its purposes, in fact, is to interpret the experience to non-veterans. But throughout the writing I have had in mind my fellow vets and I hope that my reflections will be helpful to them in their personal journeys out of the night. So I dedicate this book to Vietnam vets with profound respect and deep affection.

CHAPTER ONE:
WAR STORIES

The sun was low in the western sky, and we were almost finished with our conversation. He was an ex-Marine, a man who had become my good friend, and he and I had just spent several hours together sitting on a grassy slope in San Diego's beautiful Presidio Park, talking about the Vietnam War. My office in the Vet Center was too confining, so we often came to the park. He felt more comfortable there, surrounded by nothing more than nature's own four walls as he confronted his own personal hell.

The war stories poured out as they always did: sweeps through villages, deaths of close friends, futile attacks, firefights, the horrors of Khe Sanh, his own killing rage. As he had so many times during the weeks we had worked together, he talked about the details of his broken life: depression, rage, inability to relate to his wife, drinking, barroom fights, going from job to job, nightmares, sleeplessness—a trail of problems that always led back to Vietnam. But then something different happened—something I hadn't expected. He grew silent, looked up at the rapidly darkening sky, then shook his fist.

"God," he shouted, "you motherfucker! Where were you in Vietnam?"

We had never before discussed religion, though I knew he

was an ex-Catholic and he knew I had been an Army chaplain in Vietnam. On this particular evening, however, religion and the pain of his shattered faith caught up with him.

The real source of his rage had surfaced at last. Everything else he had told me during the preceding weeks was somehow related to that question. His anger at the government, his contempt for the military command in Vietnam, and his distrust of the Veterans Administration—none of it could compare with the rage directed heavenward that evening. For years he had lived in total spiritual eclipse. No ray of light or hope had entered his soul since Vietnam. Now, from his own dark night of the spirit, he cried out in rage and anguish. God was to blame.

As a believer, he had once "bought into the program." He had believed that God was in His heaven and all was right with the world. But in the jungles of Southeast Asia, God hadn't delivered. Where had He been? Why had his presence not been felt in Vietnam?

For countless veterans that same question remains unanswered. They often call God obscene names—bastard, motherfucker, son of a bitch—because they are convinced that He failed them at their moment of greatest need. Our teenaged soldiers of the sixties and seventies, like most Americans, had been led to believe that God would never let them down, that He would always lead them to victory over evil and preserve them in battle against the foe. In Vietnam, it didn't turn out that way. There, young men discovered that they'd "been had," and they feel terribly betrayed to this day.

If you doubt this, just listen to the stories vets tell. Or choose a book at random from the Vietnam literature, which is now abundant. The religious anguish and moral pain are inescapable; they leap out from the stories: not only the question of God's absence from Vietnam but the inversion of values, the moral confusion, indeed, the almost total corruption of the human spirit that grew out of the war.

As one who served with the soldiers as a chaplain in Vietnam and then worked with them for many years as a counselor, I am convinced that Vietnam veterans have, all along, been seeking the resolution to this profound crisis of faith and searching for answers to fundamental moral questions.

Though I served with them in Vietnam and was involved in the struggles of the bitter homecoming, the story told in this book is not mine, nor is it that of other chaplains. It is, rather, the story of those young men who served as infantrymen in combat units—"grunts," as they were called. It is the story of helicopter pilots, door gunners, and artillerymen. It is the story of the young women who served as nurses, healing the bodies—and often the spirits—of the wounded.

The spiritual journey of the vets is important for America, especially for that part of America that calls itself Christian. The veterans were forced to confront questions that most people either never consider or else consciously evade. Their story contains profound spiritual lessons for an America that desperately needs to learn the meaning of its own dark side and must discover how to find God in the midst of pervasive moral evil.

Vietnam veterans went off to a distant jungle where they were pushed to the frontiers of faith. They came back home apparently broken, in despair, a "problem" to the nation. Now, in the maturity of early middle age, they have returned from nihilism and despair, seeking and finding answers to questions that have haunted them for years. Their quest is a story of immense beauty, one that will enrich America. It is a story of the most significant spiritual journey of our time.

«« — »»

JOURNEY INTO DARKNESS: IT'S OKAY TO KILL

I had just finished mass for an infantry unit in the field. A young trooper approached somewhat sheepishly. "Hey, Chaplain," he asked quietly, "how come it's a sin to hop into bed with a *mama-san* but it's okay to blow away gooks out in the bush?" The solider was a Catholic, a former altar boy and just as horny as he could be after several months in the field with his infantry unit looking for "contact" with the enemy. He had found plenty of it—sighting down the barrel of his M-16.

Consider the question that he and I were forced to confront on that day in a jungle clearing. How is it that a Christian can, with a clear conscience, spend a year in a war zone killing people and yet place his soul in jeopardy by spending a few minutes with a prostitute? If the New Testament prohibitions of sexual misconduct are to be stringently interpreted, why, then, are Jesus' injunctions against violence not binding in the same way? In other words, what does the commandment "Thou shalt not kill" really mean?

Though I gave that young soldier an answer—as I did to others—I have never been satisfied with it. Perhaps a variety of answers is possible. One comes to mind: "It isn't a sin to blow away gooks, because most of them are evil Commies and we are fighting in Vietnam to stop the Communists from taking over the United States." If I had told him that, he wouldn't have believed it any more than I did. But it is the answer that both he and I had previously assimilated from American religious culture. The problem was that he could no longer accept it. The first crack in his religious faith was beginning to develop. Either the Gospel itself made no sense, or the people who were interpreting it to him didn't really believe it themselves.

"Thou shalt not kill" is one of the "ten big ones." In the listing of the commandments it immediately precedes the prohibition against sexual immorality. The soldier was willing to accept the latter prohibition, though he might find himself unable to follow it in the harsh circumstances of Vietnam, where sex was often no more than a release and a relief from killing and being shot at. But his religious formation, the well-spring of memory and symbol in the deepest part of his soul, also compelled him to take seriously the prohibition against killing. He knew what the commandments were, and he knew that Jesus had told His disciples to become peacemakers. He remembered the passages from the Gospel readings in which Jesus told His followers to "turn the other cheek," "put away the sword," "love your neighbor as yourself," "love one another as I have loved you." All these words had been indelibly etched in his deepest consciousness. Vietnam combat, however, had clearly thrust him into a situation in which he was forced to deny a serious norm of his religious faith and moral upbringing.

Sex with a prostitute would amount to an individual act done in partnership with one other person. No serious consequences that he could see would result, except, possibly, a case of venereal disease. On the other hand, by performing his mission as a soldier, he brought irreparable harm to the lives of others. The people he killed would remain dead. Many of the wounded would be maimed for life. Families would be permanently parted. He himself could die or be seriously wounded. He had seen his friends die and knew that their families, wives, and girlfriends experienced permanent and tragic loss. His combat mission, with its cruel and irrevocable consequences, seemed a terribly sinful activity, yet it was an activity endorsed and sponsored by a supposedly religious and moral society. He was being "scandalized" in the biblical sense by immoral acts he was told had become morally permissible. Still, somewhere deep within his soul he knew, even in the midst of combat, that this was evil.

The unsatisfactory answer that I gave him that day was the

only one that makes any moral or religious sense. It amounts to this: "You may kill others only because they are trying to kill you, for this is an act of simple, elemental self-defense." The answer is legitimate on one level but not on others. It is perhaps inescapable, given a combat situation, but it leaves much unresolved.

GUILT

Among the painful legacies of Vietnam—loss of religious faith, rage directed against God, fundamental moral questions unresolved, pervasive cynicism—one in particular is found in almost all of the stories: guilt.

Guilt has a bad name in our society. It is usually associated with unwanted and unpleasant feelings, anxieties arising from our inability to cope with our own drives and ambitions. We deal with guilt by assuring ourselves—often through some form of therapy—that guilt is an inappropriate feeling, a harmful by-product of a "punitive superego." To deal with guilt, we simply convince ourselves that we're "okay" people and then go about the business of living. But guilt reaches more deeply into the human soul than our society is willing to admit. Guilt sometimes arises from our awareness that we have, in fact, participated in evil, that we have violated conscience and acted against moral standards we had previously accepted as valid.

As the Vietnam soldiers discovered the truth about war, many experienced a profound and altogether appropriate sense of guilt. Widespread destruction of villages and peasant dwellings, and the slaughter of Vietnamese civilians affected everyone who was there. Clearly, we were simultaneously witnessing, perpetrating, and being victimized by evil. It would be strange if guilt were not almost omnipresent among vets.

The journey into unrelieved darkness of the soul begins at

that moment a person first discovers who he really is. The veneer of civilized behavior, smug feelings of righteousness, the naive belief that all's well with the world, can dissolve in a single instant of mad violence. In that unforgettable moment of discovery, a person realizes that within himself lies an almost limitless capacity for violence. Monstrous evil is no longer something he can attribute only to others. It is intrinsic to himself, something he shares with his opponents on the battlefield, with the peasants in the villages he has burned, and with his friends and relatives back home. Like a primeval Adam, he stands naked in the garden, overcome by sin. Darkness of spirit and the guilt of the human condition combine to overcome him. This is guilt in its primary, even biblical sense. It coincides with the dark night of the soul and is independent of what one actually did in Vietnam combat. It is the moment of first awareness, triggered by the monstrous evil in which one recognizes that he is no longer an onlooker but a participant.

Guilt can come in many guises. It can be a feeling, or it can be a calculated judgment—or it can arise from combination of the two. It can follow upon what one has done, did not do, or has merely witnessed. Guilt can even overcome a person simply because he has survived when others did not.

Often the significant precipitating event was so horrendous that it left a residue of many-sided guilt along with enduring psychic stress. A single terrible incident can produce emotional stress, unanswered moral questions, doubts of faith, and the dark night of the soul. The following story is particularly poignant and illustrative.

Greg Peters, a former Army platoon leader, describes just such an incident: the horror of hand-to-hand combat as his unit was overrun by North Vietnamese regulars:

> At approximately 1 a.m., while sleeping in a small two-man perimeter bunker, I was awakened to the

tremendous cracking of 120 and 240 mm rockets inside our perimeter. The noise was deafening, the light beyond spectacular. Knowing from past experience that the incoming barrage would provide cover for ground assault, I grabbed my CAR-15 and a bandolier of magazines and crawled up the perimeter berm. Upon looking over the berm, I came face-to-face with an NVA sapper not more than eighteen inches from my face. He was handsome, healthy, with soft brown eyes, wearing a green sweat cravat and carrying satchel charges to ignite our eight inch, 175 and 105 mm artillery ammo pits. I savagely screamed and emptied my magazine in his face, abruptly decapitating some mother's son. Unbelievable amounts of adrenalin flowed through my body, thoroughly intoxicating my spirit.

Behind my deceased opponent came approximately 1000 North Vietnamese running at us, blowing bugles, firing weapons and throwing Chicom grenades. There were approximately 175 G.I.s on Illingworth (the name of the fire base) and, because of our proximity to the wood line, we were absorbing the apex of the attack. It was a turkey shoot. Blasting away on automatic, changing magazines in a manic fury, bodies flying in the air.

With my barrel white hot and bleeding from multiple shrapnel wounds, true to form, my weapon jammed after about ten to twelve magazines. With my men seriously wounded and dying I assaulted the enemy using my weapon as a club. I kicked one man in the balls and as he knelt before me vomiting and grasping his groin, I broke my rifle over his skull... I continued to fight with my feet and fists and I recall crushing a small soldier's forehead with a vicious right fist. Never before or after have I felt such awesome physical strength—perhaps in my dreams.

With no weapon, I looked for grenades that were buried by debris; I found instead a case of coke cans. Being an ex-college quarterback with an arm like a cannon, I threw a full can at an enemy soldier from about five paces, flooring him with a gaping gash in his forehead. I then beat him to death with my boots and my knuckles."[1]

After an explosion ended by battle and he awoke atop a dead enemy soldier with his left cheek resting on the dead man's face, he "let out a tremendous howl and kissed him violently on his bloody cheek." He continues:

After asking God to help me, I began calling out "I'm an American, I'm an American"… I managed to obtain a new M-16 and magazines and began looking for my men amidst the piles of bodies. I would reach to pull a man up and his arm would come off in my hand. I began to weep uncontrollably and put the barrel of my weapon in dead and dying enemy soldiers' mouths ripping off three to five rounds, completely ventilating their skulls. Looking outside the perimeter, I saw two enemy carrying a wounded buddy with his arms draped over their shoulders. His feet were dragging… I drew a bead with my rifle until, weeping so intensely, I could not see them through my tears. I sat on the berm and sobbed uncontrollably. My body shook violently and my bladder exploded, drenching my lower extremities with urine.

I stalked the perimeter reciting the Act of Contrition and Hail Mary's, while stopping to kiss and bless dead Americans and Vietnamese while begging God's forgiveness for our involvement in the raw carnage that morning…

After returning from the hospital, I informed my colonel that I had "lost my punch" and spent my remaining three months as a battalion re-supply officer in a virtual spiritual stupor. *Thou shall not kill* is ringing in my ears.[2]

Real moral guilt, an appropriate response to one's actions, is a frequent and enduring residue of the war. Psychic stress may also result from the same incident that produces the guilt, but the two are not the same thing.

Philip Caputo's account of his retaliation for the losses suffered by his unit is an especially poignant confession of moral guilt. A Marine Corps platoon leader, Caputo gave an order to "get those goddamn V.C. (suspected informants)", knowing that his men would read him accurately. He wanted them dead, not captured. The lust for revenge ran high in Caputo, whose unit had suffered high losses, but an innocent boy was killed by mistake. Caputo stayed for a while and looked at the boy's corpse.

The wide, glowing, glassy eye stared at me in accusation. The dead boy's open mouth screamed silently his innocence and our guilt. In the darkness and confusion, out of fear, exhaustion and the brutal instinct acquired in the war, the Marines had made an awful mistake. They had killed the wrong man. No, not they: we. We had killed the wrong man. That boy's innocent blood was on my hands as much as it was on theirs. I had sent them out there. *My God, what have I done*? I thought. I could think of nothing else. Please, God forgive us. What have we done?[3]

Veteran rap groups and books on Vietnam abound with the telling of incidents whose natural, normal consequence is a profound, enduring sense of guilt. The problem with guilt is that it remains for years, embedded in the psyche, trapped in the center of the soul. It is essential that guilt be exorcised, but herein lies a problem we must consider. Most of us have a tendency to lessen guilt by denying the consequences of what we have done. "It really wasn't so bad after all" is one way to get rid of guilty feelings. Combat veterans can never afford themselves the luxury of rationalizations like this. What happened in the jungles and villages of Vietnam really was horrendous.

This is especially true regarding the slaughter of the innocent: old men, women, and children. Even when these deaths were unforeseen and unintended, the men who caused them were still overcome with revulsion and guilt. Sometimes they cried out for mercy and forgiveness in the horror of that moment when they first realized what they had done.

Ron Kovic describes the slaughter by his unit of a group of Vietnamese civilians, mostly children. As the Marines entered the hut they had just fired into and found that the dead and wounded were children and old people, they were overcome with shock and guilt: "Oh, God," one of them shouted. "Oh, Jesus Christ…we just shot up a bunch of kids." As the enormity of the act settled in, "the men were not moving and some of them were crying now, dropping their rifles and sitting down on the wet ground. They were weeping now with their hands against their faces. Oh, Jesus, Oh, God, forgive us."[4]

People who were not in Vietnam have difficulty imagining how ordinary young Americans—their own sons, husbands, boyfriends, the kids down the block—could kill so easily. For someone who has not been in combat, it is indeed impossible to understand the brutal transformation that takes place under fire. Some Americans made no attempt to understand what had happened in the field. They acted toward the vets in a manner that revealed their own brutality. Some antiwar protesters—for the most part young people themselves—lurked around airports and military bases, greeting returning veterans with the epithet "baby killer." The major difference between protesters and veterans, however, lay not in what each had done but in what each knew about themselves. The protesters maintained the myth of their own innocence, but the vets understood the truth about human evil.

RAGE, VENGEANCE, AND THE "GOOK SYNDROME"

The fever pitch of battle cannot be turned off like a switch. Sometimes combat rage carried over into atrocities that men have had to live with in their own memories since that day they occurred.

Taking casualties, seeing one's own men die, generates a powerful urge to take revenge. "We took casualties on the way in, and when we got there, we took apart the village" is not an uncommon story. Sometimes the consequences were horrendous.

A helicopter door gunner described to Mark Baker what happened after a particularly bad pitched battle that broke off at dawn:

> There were literally hundreds of thousands of Vietnamese fleeing the area, any way they could. Panic. The sun was up and that was it. Time to get the hell out of Dodge. This wasn't a village. It was a big swampy area. They were leaving in boats, slogging' on foot, anything. I don't know if they ran out of ammunition or what, but we were taking very little fire at that point and we were just killing everybody.
>
> It turned into a turkey shoot. They were defenseless. There were three or four light fire teams working the area. Hundreds of people were being mowed down.

Bodies were floating in the water. Insane. I was in there with the best of them. Blowing people off the boats, out of the paddies, down from the trees, for Christ's sake. Blood lust. I can't think of a better way to describe it. Caught up in the moment. I remember thinking this insane thought, that I'm God and retribution is here, now, in the form of my machine gun and the many guns that I take care of and the rockets that were firing. It was a slaughter. No better than lining people up on the edge of a ditch and shooting them in the back of the head. I was doing it enthusiastically.

You begin at that point to understand how genocide takes place. I considered myself a decent man, but I did mow those people down from my helicopter. A lot of people we were killing in the morning were the same people who had been trying to kill us that night. I tried to compensate in my head that most of the people we were wasting were the enemy. But I could appreciate in a black way that you can take anybody given the right circumstance and turn him into a wholesale killer. That's what I was. I did it, bizarre. That's what it was. It was very bizarre.[5]

Murderous rage born of a desire for revenge led to atrocity and torture. Cutting off ears and other parts of the bodies of enemy dead was a manifestation of this. A great many vets have confessed to this in private and often with considerable remorse.

Men have told me, "We found the bodies of our own men with their balls and dicks cut off and stuck in their mouths. When we found the VC motherfuckers, we did the same thing to them."

Unfortunately, many people are unable to listen to these stories with any degree of understanding. Some, on the political and religious right, can accept the notion that the "other side" committed atrocities but "not our boys." Others, of a leftist ideological persuasion, have been able to see our troops as baby killers but are unwilling to accept the truth that the Vietcong and North Vietnamese committed unbelievable atrocities themselves. War is always fueled by rage. A lust for vengeance upon the enemy is inevitable.

The slaughter of innocents sometimes occurred "because you never knew who the enemy was" or "they were all gooks." Sometimes it was just that "you had to go along with the program." If the "program" was to shoot anything that moved, innocent people died. In the words of one veteran who had taken part in several sweeps through the Delta, "We fired up the village. We really fired 'em up."

Though the language appears casual, the men who told these stories years after the events had taken place were in rap groups or talking in the privacy of an office because they could not escape from the enormity of what they had done.

The truth is that no one who picks up a weapon and uses it on a fellow human remains dispassionate. It is impossible to kill without emotional investment. The enemy must in some way be dehumanized, degraded to less than full human status. Collectively, the population of the other country must become "gooks," "Nips," "Japs," "Krauts," or "Huns." One must first hide from the full humanity of the opponent before he is able to kill him. Both sides in every war do this to each other.

In Vietnam, the Americans were often considered—and treated—as subhuman by the North Vietnamese regulars and by the Vietcong. The Vietcong, in fact, often dehumanized and terrorized their own people to keep them on the "right" side. American soldiers, for their part, had been trained to kill gooks, subhuman creatures who didn't value life in the same way we did. This "gook syndrome" led to terrible atrocities. Lee Childress tells of seeing an American solider kill an old

Vietnamese woman after she stole his spearmint gum:

> He shot her point-blank through the chest and killed her. Even now, every time I see spearmint gum it blows me right out of the fucking saddle, man...We got in more trouble for killing water buffalo than we did for killing people. That was something I could never adjust to.[6]

When he tries to find some meaning to what happened, Childress concludes:

> I think, "If you ever saw what I've seen. If you'd spent the time that I spend every fucking day of my life, going over, and over again the *why?* and the *why?* and I always know there's no answer." There's no answer anywhere. And that really scares me sometimes.[7]

Loren Baritz discusses the effects of our dehumanizing the Vietnamese.

> This question of whether we thought they were civilized had grisly side effects. This is illustrated by the case of Sven Erickson, a fictitious name given to an American GI. One month after Sven arrived in Vietnam, he became part of a five-man reconnaissance patrol. The night before they were to start, the sergeant told the others that they would take a girl with them "to have some fun." He said it would "be good for the morale of the squad." The next morning the patrol kidnapped a young woman from her mother and sister. After a day's march, with the woman carrying much of their gear, they settled in for the night. Four of the men raped the woman, but Sven, a serious Lutheran from Minnesota,

refused, despite the sergeant's questioning of his manhood, and despite accusations that he was betraying his buddies. The next day the patrol got caught in a firefight with a few guerrillas, and the sergeant gave the corporal permission to kill the woman. He stabbed her three times, twice in the chest and once in the neck. She still did not die, so he blew away part of her head with his M-16.[8]

Combat rage and the desire for vengeance were not limited to the enemy. Sometimes one's own officers were targets. No one knows how frequent this kind of killing, called "fragging," was in Vietnam—how many officers died at the hands of their own men—but it happened often enough. Usually a platoon leader or company commander had lost men through negligence or stupidity. Some wouldn't listen to advice from their troops on how to reduce casualties in combat. Sometimes the officer wanted to "John Wayne it" and led his men into needless combat. Or perhaps someone simply hated his guts. Often the justification was "It was either him or us. We told him, but he wouldn't listen." The next time the unit got into a fight, the lieutenant or captain was killed in action. Only those who killed him ever knew the truth.

It may have seemed like the only thing to do at the time, but fragging one's own officers or NCOs does not become easier to live with as the years pass and the heat of battle recedes. One man told me that he knew his company commander was going to be killed but was afraid to tell him because he feared for his own life. He watched the captain get into a chopper one day to go back to the division rear. His own troops shot down the chopper, killing the helicopter crew as well as the captain. The veteran still struggles daily with his guilt.

TERRORISM

Not all the killing took place in the heat of combat or out of a white-hot desire for vengeance. Some of it was much more cold-blooded. The Phoenix program was designed to "neutralize" the Vietcong and Communist cadre in rural areas. American advisers and South Vietnamese military and police forces were involved in it. Some of the men who took part in Phoenix became assassins, and their stories are truly unforgettable. As one of them told me, "If I live to be five hundred years old, I can never atone for what I did in Vietnam." The Phoenix story keeps coming out in the Vet Centers.

Mike Beamon, scout for a Navy Seal team, tells the story of the usual kidnapping procedure in his Phoenix operations. The victim was taken from his hootch in a matter of a minute or a minute and a half by a very efficient and well-rehearsed team. The rest of the family living in the hootch were told that if they came out they would be blown away. Beamon's job was to wait outside to cover the escape.

> I would usually sit by the hootch for about five minutes and listen and, while I was doing that, hook a grenade on the door, flatten the pin and run a fishing line across the door so if anybody opened it up, they would drop the grenade and of course they would be killed.
>
> I would sit by the doorway there and be very, very quiet and let them start mustering a bit, then I'd make a little noise outside so that they knew I was there. Once I did that, I'd leave and haul ass back to the unit to scout on the way back. If anybody came out, we could hear the grenade for about a mile if it went off. And these are like families, little kids and stuff. So it was something

you just didn't think about. You just did it. It was that second you had to cover.[9]

Beamon figured that "on some occasions the plan was to come in and assassinate a village chief and make it look like the Viet Cong did it."[10]

The context of American war stories must always be understood. Assassinations, murder and atrocity, and terrorism were committed by the other side, too. Bruce Lawlor writes about the Vietcong strategy of terror.

They used to undermine the credibility of the government and paralyze the population by selective assassinations. Selective atrocities. District chiefs, village chiefs, pro-GVN village chiefs... Disembowelment, raping your wife and children in front of you, killing your baby. We saw them. We saw people with legs hacked off... Disemboweling seemed to be a big thing. Literally pull a guy's innards out of his stomach, they'd rip his stomach open. But the sad part of it is, he doesn't die right away. Women... you know, the sky's the limit. As gruesome as you can think of things to do, they would do. Schoolteachers were a favorite target, and unfortunately a lot of the schoolteachers were idealistic young women.[11]

The journey into the night of the spirit was a journey into the ultimate degradation of the spirit: war.

STRESS AND MORAL STRAIN

Most people who served in Vietnam did not commit atrocities, kill civilians, or frag their leaders, but everyone who served "in country" was subjected to psychological stress and to something I will call moral strain. There was no such thing as a really secure rear area. No one ever knew when the next attack would come. Most infantrymen in the field were up against very good North Vietnamese regulars or the elusive Vietcong. Psychological stress was the inevitable and often the enduring effect of Vietnam. Clinical studies have shown that the heavier the combat a person experienced in Vietnam, the deeper and more prolonged the postwar "stress syndrome."

Unlike most other sources of psychological stress, that of war involves the ever-present reality of impending death, one's own or someone else's. At any time one may be called upon to kill or, conversely, be killed. Relief comes only when one has cleared hostile air space on the flight home. Because taking human life carries with it so much moral weight, combat-induced psychological stress involves a strain on the conscience, as well. This is not the same thing as personal guilt. On the contrary, it seems to be present in many cases even when a person has performed no acts for which he feels personally guilty. Just as psychological stress has continued for years after the war, so has the residue of moral strain. It is still another source of desolation of the spirit. The following story illustrates the point:

The ex-GI had served as a grunt, an infantryman with a crack unit. We sat together in his home more than ten years after he had been medically evacuated (med-evaced) from Vietnam. "The last thing I saw before I lost consciousness when I was hit was the NVA solider I killed. He wounded me and would have killed me if I hadn't got him." The vet had absolutely no guilt about killing the enemy soldier who wounded him. Clearly, this was the classic case of self-defense: kill or be killed. The man had seen a lot of combat during his tour. He had committed no atrocities, killed no civilians. He had been a practicing, church-going Christian. He had done nothing in combat that troubled him morally, but he still felt uneasy about the war. Some nameless malaise gripped him. He wasn't particularly "stressed out" in any psychological sense. He felt uneasy about "the whole Vietnam thing." He was disturbed in a moral sense.

The painful combination of stress and moral strain is often found among men who had been junior officers (platoon leaders and company commanders) or enlisted men acting as squad leaders. These men assumed tremendous responsibility—most of them at a young age. They were responsible for the lives of men they knew well and cared about very much. They often gave orders that resulted in the deaths of those who carried orders out. I can still see the pain in the eyes of the men who related the following stories.

"I can still see his face," the former Marine platoon leader told me. "He was just a kid and scared. I told him to take point, He didn't make it."

> I can still remember the radio operator's head being blown apart and then I lost consciousness. When I came to, I was the only one alive. The rest of my squad wad dead, all dead. We had been ambushed. I should have had flankers out, but I can't remember whether I did. My God, I can't remember.

Akin to this kind of stress is "survivor guilt," which is not really in a moral sense. It arises simply because one has survived combat when friends did not. Two brief examples suffice:

> "He was the best friend I ever had. We had known each other in high school and went to 'Nam together. I asked him to change guard duty with me. He got killed."

> "I was back in the rear with malaria, and my squad went out. They all got killed. God, I should've been with 'em."

Like so many others who tell similar stories, these vets did nothing consciously or deliberately to cause the deaths of their men. War, with its own terrible logic and incalculable consequences, had brought death to some and enduring wounds of the spirit to others.

Vietnam spared no one agony of spirit. The magnificent men and women who served as combat medics, nurses, and physicians—people whose efforts to save lives were truly heroic—often had a heightened awareness of the corruption of the spirit that took place in Vietnam. Lynda Van Devanter was one of them.

Like so many other nurses, Lynda spent what seemed an eternity in the madness of an evacuation hospital. Her world was that of multiple frag wounds, spurting blood, bellies blown open, screams of agony. For her, as for the other medical people, these broken bodies always remained real human beings even as they mass-produced the miracles of medicine that saved so many lives. Their ministrations included holding the hands of young men who died crying for their mothers or girlfriends. They shared with newly wounded men that terrible moment of first awareness that life would be lived from now on without legs or an arm or without sight.

The medical personnel paid a price for their sensitivity and dedication. Van Devanter writes:

> We were living by a different clock in Pleiku, and learning that chronological age has little correlation with how old some people feel. Holding the hand of one dying boy could age a person ten years. Holding dozens of hands could thrust a person past senility in a matter of weeks.[12]

It didn't take more than a few immersions in mass casualty situations for a person to realize the futility of the war. A sergeant went into seizure on the operating table and died as Van Devanter and Carl Adams, a surgeon, treated his wound. "Duty, honor, country," Carl said sarcastically. "I'd love to have Richard Nixon here for one week."[13]

Stress and moral strain were everywhere in Vietnam.

CORRUPTION OF THE SPIRIT

When compared with combat and the slaughter that took place, the corruption of other ethical standards in Vietnam seems almost insignificant. Our preoccupation with the killing and slaughter—indeed the primary moral issue—allows us to forget that the entire moral order became inverted there. Prostitution, black market, and drug addiction were rampant, but these were almost in counterpoint to the killing.

Most of the troops came to Vietnam with a basic ethical code, but in the absence of restraints upon killing, no other moral norms seemed important. Caputo's observation that "we sank into a brutish state" in the Indochina bush is accurate. It applied to everything.

The black market became so bad that a battalion commander in a troop unit at Long Binh Supply Depot issued a remarkable order. He told his officers to pass the word that any item stolen for sale on the black market should be replaced through the requisition process so the unit wouldn't be caught short of essential equipment. He had correctly assessed the situation. One of his supply sergeants boasted to me that they intended to "make the depot disappear."

During the Vietnam War drug addiction had become a problem "back in the world," as the troops referred to the States. But in Vietnam the opportunities for drug use were unlimited. Heroin was available in little vials costing about five dollars each. This was almost pure heroin, far better than the diluted stuff you paid much more for back in the world. For years after the war, VA drug treatment programs would struggle to counter the effects of those little vials of white powder.

Sexual restraint disappears very fast in a combat zone. This was certainly true in Vietnam. Women furnished relief from the incredible harshness of life. A "piece of ass" was a nice contrast to blowing someone away with your weapon. I remember the first sergeant of an infantry company who beamed with pleasure when he told me how he had discovered how much his man loved and respected him. They had just given him some money for a birthday present. The money was to be used for the "Top" to go into Vung Tau and get himself a woman. A gift certificate for a "piece of ass." In Vietnam it made some sense.

The most serious corruption went through all strata of authority-right to the top. The "war of attrition" strategy required that everyone play the numbers game. Body counts became a necessity. The troops in the field knew that enemy body counts were inflated, and they also suspected that American casualty reports were not accurate. They also knew from terrible experience that some aggressive commanders were willing to get their career tickets punched by leading troops into the right kind of combat action, even if this entailed a needless expenditure of their men's lives. The troops knew also that individuals and corporations back in the world were making big money on the war. Body counts, the military careers of their leaders, and big bucks for the folks back home—this was what the war was all about.

Thus, the legendary cynicism of Vietnam veterans developed not as a result of retrospection but of accurate perceptions of the truth engendered in the field. The war, launched amid altruistic notions that America would "bear any burden, pay any price" to hold aloft its moral beacon in the world, was held together only on the strength of lies and deception. From policy statements of presidents down to body counts in the field, truth was a casualty of war. No one knew this better than the soldiers in the field.

There is a "one-liner" evaluation of the war common among the soldiers overseas that has now become a permanent phrase in the lexicon of veterans. I think it expresses perfectly the meaning of the war in moral and religious terms. No one has ever improved upon it.

I heard it for the first time before I left the replacement center at Bien Hoa to report to my assignment with the First Cav. A young soldier with very sad eyes was on his way home a few weeks early. He had gotten an "early out" to accompany the body of his closest friend home for burial. We talked about what happened, and I told him I was sorry his friend has been killed. He looked at me and said, "Chaplain, it don't mean nothin'."

Not long afterward, one of our infantry companies had taken heavy casualties in two of its platoons. The company commander, a very able and dedicated officer, was trying to reorganize his men in the field, and to do so very quickly because of the likelihood of further combat at any moment. He asked me to talk with the men. The troops were numbed by the deaths of close friends, men who had been more than brothers to them. The only thing they could say that had any meaning for them was "It don't mean nothin'."

"It don't mean nothin'" is a statement that crosses the philosophical border into nihilism. I believe nihilism is the inevitable legacy of anyone who experiences war. To defend against this passage into a mental world devoid of meaning, societies that wage war must construct some positive *mythos* for themselves, some vision that will enable them to fight and kill while remaining sane and even morally correct—in their own eyes, at least.

Ancient tribes believed they were favored by the gods in whose name they fought. The Nazis applied Nietzsche's notion of "Superman" to themselves, opening the way for unprecedented evil, tolerable only in light of a mythic dream. Marxists believe that their own acts of endless violence acquire meaning because of a metamorphosis in humankind that will occur at some future time—the classless society in whose name the monstrous evils perpetrated along the way can be justified. To hide the truth of war from those most intimately involved—the soldiers who fight the battles—societies construct mythologies of war that glorify the bloodshed of battle. In the myths of war, soldiers become larger than life, and as warriors they enter into the mythic world of heroes.

American warriors, no less than those of ancient tribes, take with them into battle a cult of war that preserves them from the nihilism that arises the moment one grasps the truth about war. In Vietnam, the defense mechanism failed.

"It don't mean nothin'" proclaims the death of a powerful national mythology. Because of the long connection between the American myth and traditional biblical religion, the vets' newfound nihilism acquires an even deeper significance in our society—a religious one. "Where was God in Vietnam?" becomes the only legitimate religious question one can ask after saying, "It don't mean nothin'."

To a greater extent than we would like to admit, the vets' moral insights in this regard are superior to those of most other commentators, political leaders, and pundits who talk and write about the war. People like Nixon and Kissinger, for example, write about the war almost without reference to the people who suffered from it. The only issues important to them are global ones; they ignore the terrible and immediate impact of war on the lives of people. However much they may perform a service by placing the war in a global context, our sages and leaders remain essentially amoral with respect to war because they are blind to its cost in human terms. The vets, on the other hand, never lose sight of that terrible cost. For this reason their accounts are seldom free of moral strain and psychic stress.

The difference in attitude and moral awareness held by our leaders on the one hand and by troops in the field on the other was brought home to me one day shortly after I heard a speech given by President Nixon on Armed Forces Radio. The president had intoned solemnly that we were in Southeast Asia "fighting for peace." A short time later a grunt who was spending a few days in a rear area approached me, his face aglow with mirth. "Chaplain," he asked, "did you hear Nixon?" I replied that I had. "It's all bullshit," he said. "Fighting for peace is like fucking for virginity."

Indeed, his insight was correct. Combat operations in Vietnam were as likely to bring about peace as sexual intercourse was to restore lost virginity. To believe that war brings peace is a delusion. To act upon that delusion is the final corruption of the human spirit.

DARK NIGHT: THE RELIGIOUS EXPERIENCE

Religion and morality are not the same thing, but they are related. All the world's great religions have been connected with some kind of ethical code. Most of the men and women who served in Vietnam had been members of a Christian church. Whether or not they were personally devout, their understanding of religion was usually in Christian terms. For this reason, their spiritual journey can be understood only within the context of Christian assumptions about religion and life.

American Christianity reflects biblical moral teaching and principles derived from Western philosophical ethics, but it does so with heavy moralistic emphasis and tone—a heritage handed down from colonial times and still deeply rooted in American religious thinking. Even churches that did not develop out of the Protestant Reformation have been influenced by the central themes of Calvinism, that strain of Protestantism brought to our shores by the pilgrims.

Two ideas in particular are significant. The first is the belief that faith and grace must bring about an inner assurance—the feeling—that one is saved. The second is that material prosperity is a sign of God's blessing. These ideas have had a profound impact on church doctrine and practice, but their scope is not limited to the churches; they have also exerted a major influence on secular thinking and American history.

These two notions have important consequences: we Americans must not only *be* moral and religious, but we must also *feel* that we are. This feeling amounts to an inner conviction that we have found favor with God. God's favor, in turn, results in prosperity, success, and material blessings. All this, of course, is not our doing but is God's free gift to us. In this way we use the language and imagery of the Bible as the basis for a distinctively Protestant/American kind of faith and practice. Authentic biblical religion does not depend at all on good feelings and material prosperity, but a great many Americans believe that it does.

All this is germane to the Vietnam experience, because in our culture war is impossible without this religious underpinning. It is what allows a soldier to remain sane and convinces him he is morally correct while he kills. It is what gives the *feeling* that "God is on his side." This feeling is his only defense against nihilism. It is a world view that "grips him in the guts" and satisfies his mind at the same time. Without it, the most he can say about war is that "it don't mean nothin'."

A great many Vietnam veterans have become religious agnostics or are now hostile to religion because they took seriously what they learned in Bible classes or in the parochial schools about killing. War stories describe very clearly what happened to the religious feelings of these warriors. Combat shattered their Calvinist/American worldview. They experienced themselves in a new way—not as moral, religious, blessed, but as both perpetrators and victims of a massive and mindless violence. The sustaining rationale drawn from traditional American religion collapsed in the face of the Vietnam reality. They could no longer *feel* religious or moral; therefore, in their own judgment, they *were* not.

It is important to remember that the men and women who went off to war in Southeast Asia were not theologians and philosophers. They were ordinary Americans. For the most part they were high school graduates and college dropouts. Ethnic minorities were represented in disproportionate numbers among the combat troops. The core of the military was, as always, the professional officers and enlisted personnel, highly trained and motivated. Some college graduates and even people with advanced degrees entered the service, usually becoming officers through the OCS program. Add to this the doctors and nurses and a sprinkling of lawyers and clergy. But for the most part Vietnam veterans were blue-collar Americans. Their average age in combat was slightly over nineteen. They were plunged into a religious experience for which they were totally unprepared.

Their religious and moral experience amounted to an unprecedented and totally unexpected deadening of the soul. The spirit went numb. The reservoir of moral resources ran dry. The "juice and joy" feeling that Americans believe to be the essence of religion and spirituality was no longer possible for large numbers of Vietnam veterans. A terrible bleakness had overwhelmed the soul.

Moreover, Vietnam combat sowed seeds of doubt about the foundations of faith. Not only the American religious experience but authentic biblical faith was called into serious question. Where indeed was God in Vietnam? Why did He allow death to be so capricious and brutal? Could He do nothing about the slaughter? Is religious faith possible after Vietnam? Can life ever have meaning again?

American Christianity rests no more comfortably with questions like these and with intellectual doubt than it does with the absence of good feeling. Severe doubt about the very foundation of faith only worsens the bleakness caused by the departure of religious feeling. The veterans knew no precedent for this kind of doubt, nor were they aware of any guidance available. Only one thing made sense: "It don't mean nothin'."

For great numbers of veterans, duty in Vietnam was a journey into spiritual darkness—the very darkest night of the soul. For many veterans the darkness remains to this day; but for others it has begun to lift. With Vietnam still frozen in their souls, some vets have now begun to "cut themselves a set of orders out of 'Nam." They have charted their own course for a journey out the night.

The story of their journey out of the night is important not only to the veterans themselves but to all Americans. The society that sent its young sons and daughters into a caldron of violence and watched them return confused, angry, and weary of spirit must now learn from their experience. Among the lessons America must learn is how to weather the winter of the spirit. A culture that voids spiritual bleakness and denies its own dark corners must somehow learn that the dark night of the soul can be an entry point into a transcendent spiritual light.

CHAPTER TWO: BACK IN THE WORLD

DEROS: DELIVER US FROM EVIL

In Vietnam you lived only for DEROS, your "date of estimated return from overseas." If you were in the Army, Air Force, or Navy, your DEROS was one year from the day you landed in country. For Marines it was thirteen months. The name of the game was to stay alive until the day you once again be "back in the world." If you were at all religious in your thinking, DEROS was what you prayed for when you said the Lord's Prayer petition "deliver us from evil." DEROS was all about deliverance from evil. It meant first of all that your own life would no longer be in moment-by-moment jeopardy. It meant also that you would be liberated at last from the necessity of killing; and that your own soul would have lifted from it the burden of its newly discovered capacity for limitless violence. DEROS meant deliverance from the moral as well as the geographic wilderness of the Vietnam jungle.

The notion of DEROS carried with it the sum of all your expectations for the future. You dreamed about how it would be when you returned to the old neighborhood, the girlfriend, the old buddies. Your parents would be proud of you. The welcome would be marvelous.

For most vets, the dreams never quite materialized. They were safe physically, but not psychologically and not spiritually. Though no longer compelled to wander through the hostile Indochina bush, their forced march was now a lonely trek through the wilderness of their own troubled souls. The problem was subtle, not easily understood at first. Things were the same back in the world, but the soldiers had changed irrevocably—in ways they would discover painfully in the years to come. Young men who were nineteen and twenty when they went to Vietnam had aged a lifetime in a year. Boys whose most troublesome moral problem had been what to do about frequent sexual arousal returned from the combat zone as old men, jaded by images of death, engulfed in a lonely state of spiritual darkness.

The speed of it all was overwhelming. There was simply no transition period. Unless a man was wounded and medically evacuated to a military hospital, he stayed with his unit until DEROS. He was then pulled out of the line, separated from the closest friends he had ever had, and sent to a replacement center in a rear area to wait a flight home. He returned from Vietnam the say way he arrived, as an isolated individual. After a flight through either Okinawa or Alaska, the plane landed at Travis or McChord Air Force bases on the West Coast. When the plane touched down on American soil, the cabin erupted in cheers.

A taxi trip to the nearest commercial airport, another flight, and the serviceman was home. If he had completed his time in the service, he was also discharged before he caught the flight home. If he still had time remaining, he went on leave before reporting to his next duty station.

«« — »»

WELCOME HOME

I left Vietnam and thirty-seven and a half hours later I was home. Home, in the middle of fucking November, drizzle and 32 degrees. No transition, fucking weird.[14]

With no period of time allowed to "debrief" or work through the emotional turmoil that was to be Vietnam's enduring legacy, the veteran still expected to resume life as it had been before his combat experience. But this was not to be. Faces of the dead intruded upon his consciousness—sometimes the haunting faces of Vietnamese women and children. He was at last forced to confront his real feelings about the death and suffering he had known in Vietnam. Shock waves of grief, anger, and revulsion now engulfed him. His faith remained shattered, guilt deepened, psychic stress and moral strain were aggravated. The promised "light at the end of the tunnel" remained as elusive at home as it had been overseas.

At first no one knew why the past remained to haunt both waking hours and nighttime dreams, though the answer is quite easy to understand: repression. A soldier's job is to survive, to keep himself and his friends alive—by killing. In Vietnam any feelings that interfered with the business of killing and staying alive had to be banished from consciousness. But now, back home, with danger removed, the vet's normal emotional process resumed. Fear, grief, anger, and guilt, the emotional residue of combat, now surfaced. The veteran, whose average age upon return was slightly more than twenty, had to face it all alone.

The primary mission back in the world became emotional survival. A strange gulf separated the veteran from his parents. Mom just couldn't understand; Dad might have understood, but he didn't seem willing to listen. If the girlfriend or young wife was still waiting, she was somehow in a "different place." There was no way to share Vietnam with her. How could the intimacy of a sexual relationship endure the even greater intimacy of combat memories?

Even old friends, the kids down the block, high school buddies, or college friends couldn't relate to the vet anymore. The classic dialogue with old friends went something like this: "Haven't seen you for a while. Where've you been?" "Vietnam." "Oh," followed by an embarrassed silence. No one wanted to listen. Perhaps no one could stand to listen. Sometimes people asked cruel questions for which there is no possible response: "How does it feel to kill?" or "How many people did you kill?" All this simply reinforced the vet's isolation. But the worst was when people really didn't care what he'd been through.

> I went home straight from California to O'Hare Airport in Chicago. I got home about three in the morning. Everybody in the house got up and said hello. Then they all went back to sleep. At 8:30 when my father left for work, he woke me up to say, "Listen, now that you're home, when are you going to get a job?" I packed up and left. I haven't been home since.[15]

Hostility from old friends became increasingly common as the war dragged on and opposition at home grew. Going out for a few beers with people who hadn't been to Vietnam became an ordeal. It didn't take long for the war to come up in a conversation fueled by alcohol; there is a limit to the number of times anyone can hear it said that he must have been crazy to go or, even worse, to be reminded that he is some kind of moral outcast. For most veterans the line of least resistance became simply not to mention anything about the service or the war.

The attitudes of old friends weren't the only problem. Vets who had not yet been able to change from uniform to civilian clothes were often spat upon by strangers during their first hours home. A short haircut or any other indication of veteran status could—and often did—lead to spitting, that ancient and honored mode of reviling the despised among us.

Lynda Van Devanter recalls her arrival back in the world. Landing at Travis Air Force Base in California in the early hours of the morning, she was herded onto a bus and driven to the Oakland Army Terminal at about 5:00 a.m. Her flight home was from San Francisco International Airport, more than twenty miles away. With no commercial transportation available at that hour, she tried to hitchhike—the only way you could get around in Vietnam. Wearing her uniform, she watched drivers whiz by her, some slowing only to give her the finger or yell obscenities. One driver threw a carton of trash, another a half-empty can of soda.

> Finally two guys stopped in a red and yellow Volkswagen bus. The one on the passenger side opened his door. I ran to the car, dragging the duffel bag and other luggage behind me. I was hot, tired, and dirty.
>
> "Going anywhere near the airport?" I asked.
>
> "Sure am," the guy said. He had long brown hair, blue eyes framed by wire-rimmed glasses, and a full curly beard. There were patches on his jeans and a peace sign on his T-shirt. His relaxed, easy smile was deceptive.
>
> I smiled back and lifted my duffel bag to put it inside the van. But the guy slammed the door shut. "We're going past the airport, sucker, but we don't take Army pigs." He spit on me. I was stunned.
>
> "Fuck you, Nazi bitch," the driver yelled. He floored the accelerator and they both laughed uncontrollably as the VW spun its wheels for a few seconds, throwing dirt and stones back at me before it roared away.
>
> The drivers of other passing cars also laughed.[16]

The nurse who had looked into the agonized faces of so many dying men now found herself the object of "the look" directed at her by passing drivers.

> The look would start around the eyes, as if they were peering right through me. Their faces would harden into stone. I was a pariah, a non-person so low that they believed they could squash me underfoot; I was as popular as a disease and as untouchable as a piece of shit...
>
> Around 10:30 a.m., when I had given up hope and was sitting on my duffel bag, a passing driver shouted three words that perfectly illustrated my return to the world:
>
> "Welcome home, asshole!"[17]

Like countless vets, Lynda Van Devanter became aware on the very day of her homecoming that she had become a stranger in her own land.

College classes provided painful for many, especially as the antiwar movement grew. Faculty as well as students took their shots at veterans—obvious and easy targets for anyone who wanted to protest. The vets had achieved the warrior's dream, entry into the realm of myth and symbol, but it wasn't exactly the sort of realm they'd originally had in mind.

> I went back to school that September. I paid my own way to school. I didn't want to get my GI benefits because I didn't want nobody to know that I was a veteran. I was ashamed, because everybody in the U.S. hated GIs for being in the Nam. I was trying to hide myself.
>
> I thought maybe if I go to school I can adjust. I go to school and they're saying, "Those fucking GIs over in Vietnam." The professors would shake their heads. "It's

a shame those GIs are over Vietnam killing innocent people." I wouldn't say nothing.[18]

Men who had been wounded, lost limbs, or been disfigured as a result of combat injuries were also targets. An ex-Marine related to a rap group that he had been proud to join the corps. He had given up a promising college career to enlist. Vietnam was the place to be; they were "passing out balls" over there. But once in country, he was like everyone else; he lived only for DEROS.

After a few weeks out in the bush, he got hit, shot in the face and blinded. He almost died, but modern medical science pulled him through. The return home wasn't what he had anticipated, but he made it, and after months in Navy hospitals, he was released. Plastic surgery had repaired much of the damage, but he would forever carry the evidence of a massive and devastating injury. He would also carry the psychic scar that went with the wound. Isolated and depressed, he began to respond to professional therapy and to some real friendship.

He decided to return to college. Courage overcame his fear of going back to school as a blinded veteran. Not long after he had enrolled, he became involved in a discussion of tax breaks for blinded veterans. One of his classmates remarked pointedly that he opposed the measure because it "would endorse what is going on over there." Years later, after he successfully completed a master's degree at a local university, the blind ex-Marine told the rap group that he "never felt like a veteran."

Cruelty of this kind was not uncommon; it was often worse than this. Amputees and paraplegic veterans have reported that when asked how they were injured, they responded truthfully, "In Vietnam."

The reply was etched forever in memory: "Good; you got what you deserved."

THE UNTAINTED: THOSE WHO STAYED HOME

Parents, elders, teachers, and religious leaders were unable to provide any guidance to the vets because they had no comparable experience themselves. Veterans of previous wars had certainly known combat, but combat for them had through the years taken on a special meaning. They had filtered their own painful memories through a peculiar prism that the mind uses to reinterpret combat, to give it some sort of mystical value. They used this filtering mechanism to preserve their sanity, their moral integrity, and their sense of religious righteousness.

As difficult as it was to relate to their elders, however, Vietnam GIs faced quite another, far worse problem with people in their own age group. Their peers, especially those higher on the ladder of education and wealth, shunned them. Vets were considered moral outcasts, baby killers, perpetrators and atrocities. One did not associate with such people and retain one's own sense of self-worth. The message from these guardians of America's conscience was clear: Vietnam veterans were pariahs. They were immoral and evil people. To their own peer group, those with whom they had grown up, with whom they shared the same Little League games, rock music, sexual adventures, they had become non-persons.

Of course, not everyone who stayed home lacked compassion for the vets. Even many of those who participated in the anti-war protests had suffered personal loss as a result of the war. Brothers and friends had been killed, maimed, injured, or captured. Family after family experienced violent rifts; fathers and sons, brothers and sisters were turned against one another. In many of these instances, the loss, pain and personal compassion triggered heated antiwar sentiments at a social and political level. Protesters might go home at night to care for a disabled veteran who was a loved one.

Tacit disapproval and fear also played a role. Many did not know how to react to a vet who had seen hell. So silence and awkwardness formed their responses—perhaps equally as painful to vets as the overt hostility they did experience.

But as a society, America without a doubt abused those who came home from the war. We were not proud of what happened in Vietnam; how could we be proud of our vets?

The result was predictable. No longer feeling integral to their society, vets began to seek comradeship only among themselves. They became distant from non-vets and bound to each other by the discovery of the violence within their own souls. Each had confronted the beast within himself. Each could say, "I'm an animal."

The isolation imposed on the veterans further reinforced the idea that everyone else in American society was innocent, that blood had not sullied those who stayed home. During the early seventies the American people immersed themselves in this kind of self-righteousness, thus insulating themselves from the beast in their own hearts. The man who returns from combat and says, "I'm an animal," knows a certain truth about himself. The person who taunts him or cannot bear to hear his story is simply hiding from the truth.

The anger that grew up against American society was so deep and widespread among veterans that it soon became legendary. At its root lay the recognition of unacknowledged hypocrisy. The society that refused them reentry was the same one that had sent them off to kill. Was this an innocent land, untouched by malevolence, where citizens could treat its soldier sons like mutant offspring? Were the protestors, the college students, and the draft evaders the legitimate heirs of moral superiority? The veterans thought not, but no one would listen.

The winter of the spirit deepened back in the world. Veterans, held at bay from society, lived on in the night of the soul that had descended on them in Vietnam. The darkness was characterized by a sense of collective guilt that no one would share. Regardless of what a person had done in Vietnam, he felt tainted by having been there at all.

OLDER VETS: THE LIFERS BACK HOME

Rejection by the innocents might have been bearable had the vets been able to gain access into another segment of American society: its pantheon of heroes who had gone to war before them. The young GIs had gone into battle inspired by John Wayne movies and tales of their fathers' exploits in the big war ("World War II, the one we won"). Most of them wanted to come back in glory, welcomed into the ranks of America's honored warriors. That welcome never took place. Young vets discovered that combat alone didn't provide entry into the clan of the warrior elite; you had to share the clan's mind-set, as well.

World War II vets, especially as they assembled in such organizations as the Veterans of Foreign Wars (VFW) and the American Legion, presented a formidable challenge to the Vietnam generation. The older men all seemed to "think like lifers." "Lifers" in the Viet vet lexicon refers to career military, officers and senior NCOs who were in for twenty or more years. The word connotes more than a career spent in military service, however. Lifers tended to "buy into the bullshit" in Vietnam. They planned and executed the strategy that cost lives, and even worse, they seemed to do so without question. They kept the troops in line (which was their job), but they seemed immune to the questions and doubts that tortured those troops. They often seemed perfectly willing to sacrifice the lives of their men to get their career tickets punched. One former grunt told me that while he was in Vietnam he "hated lifers more than the enemy." This was not an uncommon emotion.

To the Vietnam vets' way of thinking, VFW and American

Legion members thought, talked, and acted like lifers. In fact, they found this true of most World War II veterans. Even men who had enlisted and served only for the duration during World War II, men who couldn't wait to get out of the service and who never considered a career in the military, still thought and talked like lifers. Vietnam vets couldn't accept these older veterans. And the feeling was mutual.

In fact, most Americans think like lifers. Our cultural understanding of war, patriotism, the place of other nations in the world, and especially our own sense of self-righteousness are the very basis of "lifer" attitudes. The Vietnam veterans themselves had cut their teeth on the lifer mind-set. The same attitudes and outlooks they had taken from their fathers had led most of them into the military so they could fight a war on their own. *It was the war itself that had changed them.*

I remember when in one evening rap group the subject of the VFW came up. Opinion was divided between "Fuck those old drunks" and "Let's all join up and take over the post." One vet decided to test the latter hypothesis and left the meeting early to go to the nearest VFW post. He returned not long afterward in a rage. He said he had been refused a membership application, and he wanted to round up some of the troops in the rap group and go back to "beat the shit out of the motherfuckers." Cooler heads prevailed. One other vet went with him, and after some discussion with whoever was in charge at the VFW post, both were invited to join.

The older men considered the Vietnam crop of vets "crybabies," "pussies," and downright unpatriotic. They were unwilling to listen to what Vietnam vets were saying about the war. The gulf between them represented far more than just a generation gap. For all veterans, war is the decisive experience of a lifetime. Combat memories intrude upon consciousness throughout the rest of one's life, shaping attitudes and feelings, influencing decisions, even conditioning behavior in subtle ways. But war's prism is set according to certain mental contours; it is located within a particular moral/religious/philosophical context. For the two groups of veterans, this inner landscape was vastly different. The words that undergird war are ever the same—God, country, patriotism, morality—but for the younger vets the meanings of those words have changed.

For America's newest crop of veterans, war was something much different from what it had been for their warrior ancestors. Because they placed war in a different philosophical and moral context, they were denied access to the sacred pantheon of warriors. They did not understand the additional price that must be paid to attain apotheosis. One had to "buy into the program" as well as fight a war. In our culture, war is a glorious undertaking in behalf of a morally righteous cause. Americans are simply unwilling to believe that "war sucks" or that "combat is a motherfucker." Distanced from the older generation and from their own peers, the vets became extremely bitter and isolated.

THE VET AS SCAPEGOAT

Rather than alter out mental landscape, situating anew the religious/moral/philosophical context of war, American society chose instead an ancient remedy—it made scapegoats of the veterans.

Scapegoating goes back to biblical times. When the people of Israel celebrated the Day of Atonement, the high priest laid his hands upon a goat while confessing the sins of the people. Symbolically laden with the sins of Israel, the goat was expelled into the desert. Modern, non-biblical societies no longer select animals as scapegoats. They choose instead from among their own members. The sins of the people are no longer confessed, but denied. Whatever collective evil has made it necessary for the society to seek a scapegoat is attributed entirely to the scapegoat. Modern people assert their own innocence by convicting the scapegoat. The ancient confession of sin is replaced in our time by a protestation of general innocence, the sin being laid—really, not symbolically—upon the few.

Vietnam veterans became in this way a modern equivalent of public sinners. They deeply resented the role. Enforced isolation for the sake of preserving the public's innocence was unacceptable.

Complete reintegration into society was—and remains—a major goal of the veterans movement, but this was never intended to be completely on society's terms. Radically altered perceptions, emotional turmoil, loss of innocence, dark night of the spirit—these were the enduring legacies of Vietnam. The soldiers who fought the war could never understand why those who stayed home were unwilling to share this bitter inheritance with them. The vets knew, as did everyone else in the United States, that every moment of the Vietnam War depended on the consent of the people. Clearly the majority of our people became morally uncomfortable with the war. The nation was able to ease its conscience by distancing the veterans, relegating them to the role of society's sinners. The scarlet letter was theirs alone to wear.

Religious America, Christian America, was complicit in two assaults on the faith of its young veterans. The first was perpetrating the war itself while tolerating the endorsements and mythology that surround war in our culture. The second was scapegoating the veterans, laying full responsibility for what happened on their shoulders. Scapegoating amounted to an implicit recognition that the war was evil. Like Pontius Pilate and Lady Macbeth, the American people washed their hands of the war, assuaging their own consciences by treating the veterans as moral outcasts.

Subtly isolated, scapegoated, and separated, the veterans

continued the spiritual journey they had begun in Vietnam. "It don't mean nothing'" became a pervasive attitude, a way of life. God had abandoned them in Vietnam. Their people—God's people—rejected them back home. The terrible dark night of the soul deepened. No one understood; no one cared to listen. With few exceptions, American Christian churches, having neither the spiritual resources themselves nor the interest, made no attempt to reach out or to assist the vets.

SPIRITUAL JOURNEY IN A SECULAR LAND

Deliverance of the vets from inner darkness could have begun sooner if America had demonstrated concern for them in some tangible ways. The spiritual dimension of life both grows out of and encompasses the secular realm. Though the two domains can sometimes be viewed separately, they are inseparable in fact and intertwined in all of life.

Economic, social, and political realities impinged upon the vets, determining the course of their journey back home. The picture was bleak. Confronted from every quarter with hostility, rejection, or at the very least, apathy, there was no alternative for most but to "drop out" emotionally. Thousands took leave of organized society and headed for the wilderness areas of America, where many still live alone. Most vets remained physically in cities, towns, and rural communities but lived a double life. Vietnam remained the decisive event in their lives, shaping attitudes and behavior, but they were convinced that no one else understood, so they banished Vietnam from the consciousness. They tried to pretend it never happened.

Vietnam remained for countless vets an "undigested lump of life." Their dreams were combat nightmares—when sleep was possible. Wooded areas conjured up memories of patrols that cost lives. Crowds were intolerable; loud noises sent them searching for cover in parking lots and city streets. Wives, wondering what had happened to the carefree young men of prewar days, divorced them. Some vets walked off job after job, tired of the "hassle." Employers heard stories about them; finding jobs became even more difficult. Alcohol and drugs, always available, were frequently used. Barroom fights and violent behavior provided easy outlets for rage and aggression, which seemed somehow never to diminish. Prison and chronic depression claimed others. Suicide became for many the final escape from the 'Nam.

No one really knows how many lives were disrupted. Estimates used in support of the nationwide VA Outreach Program indicated that one in five people who had served in Vietnam suffered from what was then called "post Vietnam syndrome." Other estimates put the number at one in three combat veterans. These estimates have been revised upward on the basis of more recent studies, but as we shall see, clinical definitions are misleading. The undeniable fact is that a very large number of Vietnam veterans were compelled to sneak back into society because of the cruel, inhumane treatment they received upon their return, and for years veterans have borne a grudge against the American people for the shabby welcome home they received.

The release of pent-up rage attracted public notice in 1981 when the Iranian hostages were released. Vietnam veterans, like all Americans, were delighted that the hostages were home safe. But the vets told the country that they resented very deeply the heroes' welcome given to "kidnap victims," while they themselves had been compelled to slink home in disgrace.

The flood of emotion in connection with the "National Salute" and the dedication of the Vietnam War memorial in Washington in 1982, the second "National Salute" on Veterans Day 1983, and the tenth anniversary events in 1985 provided some catharsis for feelings long suppressed.

JOBS

Southern California attracts all kinds of people. It's a place to get a new start when things don't work out back home. During the 1970s, Vietnam veterans came West by the thousands. Many of those I encountered had no job and no place to stay. Their only possession was the hope that somehow the future would be different.

One man had been turned down for several jobs, had run out of places to stay, and had ended up sleeping on the beach at Santa Monica. I asked him why he had come to California with no connections and no promise of a job. He asked me if I had ever tried sleeping on the beach in New Jersey during the winter. I got the message. Like most, he was very bitter that his country was willing to pay him and to provide the necessities and even the amenities of life as long as he was needed to kill "gooks," but now that his services were no longer required, all doors were closed. He was, he felt, less likely than his non-veteran peers to find a job. He sensed that employers were afraid of him. And he was right. Many were.

We ran a job-placement service in the Veterans Administration Office in Los Angeles. State employment agencies each had at least one veteran specialist whose sole responsibility was to place veterans in work. Despite the best efforts of a lot of dedicated people, the response on the part of employers was indeed disgraceful. Employers would tell us "off the record" that they didn't really want veterans because of the well-publicized drug problems and because of the stereotype of the kill-crazy Vietnam veteran. Most of the time we had no choice but to send out a number of veterans for the same job. Often a non-vet landed the job.

Public agencies were supposed to honor veterans' preference points. Federal agencies complied for the most part, but local agencies often evaded the regulations. I remember a personnel officer of the city of Los Angeles telling me that he had no intention of giving veterans preference and challenging me to do anything about his decision. It took a Vietnam veterans committee, established by Mayor Bradley himself, to accomplish much in the city departments of Los Angeles.

I remember one veteran I unsuccessfully tried to place through the VA and state agencies. During a conversation with him, another vet, a drug addict, very "stressed out" but employed, stopped by my desk. I explained the problem to him. He told us that his mother-in-law ran a small business and she just might have a job available. She did. The vet got it. After that I cultivated more mother-in-law type connections.

Though the vets focused much of their anger on the Veterans Administration—some of it well deserved—for the problems they encountered in obtaining benefits, in the matter of jobs the VA did what it could but was largely frustrated by private-sector employers. Much lip service was paid to hiring Vietnam Veterans: "Don't forget, hire a vet" was a popular slogan of the time. Most of it, however, was hypocritical. Vietnam vets were at a disadvantage in finding jobs because of the widespread presumption that they were baby killers and junkies. Employers, many of them World War II veterans, could talk a marvelous line about the tremendous "sacrifices these boys have made serving their country," but they wouldn't think of hiring one, because it might not be good for business. The vets knew what was going on and said so: "It's all bullshit." It was.

THE VETERANS ADMINISTRATION

The Veterans Administration certainly deserves mention in any discussion of conditions "back in the world." It provides medical treatment for service-connected injuries and illness. Medical treatment includes psychiatry and other mental health services. The VA also pays monetary compensation for injuries or illness incurred while in the service. Finally, it pays GI Bill educational benefits.

Equally important is the VA's function as a symbol of the government's concern for the veteran. The VA's motto is taken from President Lincoln's pledge in 1865 to bind up the nation's wounds and "to care for him who shall have borne the battle, and for his widow, and his orphan." Veterans of all wars know this and quite rightly regard the VA as a weather vane of America's interest in them. The agency carries with it the legal obligation to perform its task, but it also bears a moral responsibility to embody Lincoln's promise. It both performs its symbolic function and exercises its moral responsibility in and through the way it carries out its legal duties.

VA rating boards, located in regional offices across the country, were a major irritant to vets. Rating boards, comprised of one medical doctor and two specialists in VA law, determine eligibility for monetary and medical benefits. Their primary function is to determine whether a veteran's injury or illness is connected to his military service. If "service connected," the board then determines the amount of monetary compensation due. Rating boards are autonomous. Their decisions are reversible only by the Board of Veterans Appeals in Washington.

Boards differ greatly both in level of skill and in compassion. They range from very good to capricious and mean spirited. The following story illustrates the kind of rating board that gives the VA a bad name:

A vet, married with two small children, 60 percent disabled from wounds received in Vietnam, was desperate for work. He was not considered "employable" by anyone who interviewed him for a job. A provision in the VA rating code provides that a veteran may be paid at the rate of 100 percent if he has a combination of disabilities totaling 60 percent and if the VA decides that he is unemployable because of these disabilities. The distinction is important because a family can live on 100 percent compensation but not on 60 percent. In this case, the rating board decided that he was employable and refused to pay him the full benefit. The board refused to accept documentation from five or six employers who stated in writing their reason for refusing him employment.

I set up an interview for him with the VA personnel officer who refused to hire him. I then told the rating board of the decision made by their own personnel office, and they still refused to pay the unemployability benefit. Only the threat of press coverage and the director's persuasion changed their minds.

For the most part, the VA does its best to pay benefits properly and on time, but this case illustrates an attitude of mind sufficiently widespread on the part of VA employees to warrant the anger directed against the agency.

Most of the complaints against the VA are directed at its medical system. Vietnam veterans hold in special contempt the agency's mental health services. While these have improved somewhat during the past five or six years, they were inadequate and often useless during the period immediately after the war.

Images of death, often of atrocities, haunted the veterans. The classic story, recounted so often that it became a paradigm, is that of a vet, finally overcome by emotions connected with his combat memories, who approaches a VA psychiatrist. More often than not the doctor was still in training as a psychiatric resident. He was usually about the same age as the veteran and had not been in the service. Nothing in the doctor's training or experience had prepared him to take combat seriously as a source of mental or emotional distress. Moreover, the doctor always felt that he knew better than the patient what caused the symptoms, and he was not about to learn anything from disheveled malcontents who complained about war. Often the vets felt the doctor seemed uncomfortable in their presence. "He was probably an antiwar protester" was a common judgment.

At any rate, as the story unfolds, the doctor goes through the intake interview in a very professional manner. He focuses on problems of early childhood, relationships with parents, sexual development, etc. At no point does the doctor take the combat experience seriously. In fact, this seems to be the one issue that can't be raised in the interview. If mentioned, it is brushed aside as irrelevant. The only problem the veteran really needs to deal with is considered taboo. The story usually ends with the veteran walking out in anger after a very frustrating interview. "Fuck you, Doc" was a common parting comment.

There were, of course, some marvelous, dedicated therapists who truly understood the dimensions of the problem and really tried to help, but these were so few as to be truly notable.

Myra MacPherson describes the experience of a veteran named Jerry. "I'd be walking down a road and just start cryin' like a baby. Just all lonesome inside"[19]

Jerry, like countless other veterans, blamed his feelings on himself, never considering Vietnam the problem. He sought help and received the standard treatment: "They never asked you much questions. Wouldn't talk about Vietnam, and they never asked me nothin' about it."[20]

The commonly accepted stereotype of the Vietnam veteran blaming society and using Vietnam as an excuse is incorrect. MacPherson rightly concludes that Jerry was among the overwhelming silent majority who refused to blame his war experience. And no one helped him to see otherwise."[21]

MacPherson allows her anger to well up when she hears stories like Jerry's. She writes:

The obtuseness, the downright stupidity in the way troubled veterans were treated a decade ago, is one of the greatest indictments of our society, the medical profession in general, and the VA in particular.[22]

For many vets, the inability of the VA mental health services to come to grips with combat-related problems was the final straw. They felt they were not taken seriously by the one agency mandated to help them. They had been "fucked up" by the war, but the agency was unwilling or unable to deal with what was for them the war's major legacy. Their isolation was complete.

Some may think I am being too hard on the VA mental health services of that period, but hostility among veterans was so widespread that it became necessary to set up "storefront" centers to provide readjustment counseling. Though these were VA facilities and the counselors VA employees, the Vet Centers could not be located in any existing VA building. Regulations required that they be placed in the community and away from VA facilities. Though this was not "cost-effective," it was crucial to the success of the program. The reason was clear: Vietnam veterans hated the VA and would not have approached the centers under any other circumstances.

The first rap group I conducted in the San Diego Vet Center illustrates this point. The center was located a full thirteen miles from the VA medical center and about five miles from the regional office. It was located in an old building in downtown San Diego. Distance from the hated agency lent some enchantment but didn't completely solve the problem. The discussion for the first twenty minutes of our initial Tuesday evening rap group centered around my "game." Even though I was a veteran, the fact was that I now worked for the VA. Was I really FBI or CIA? Was I pimping for the VA? "What kind of motherfucker would work for the VA?"

We decided that the only way to find out about my game would be to get about the business of talking about the war.

Some of the men in that first rap group are now close friends, and we laugh about that unforgettable session. Vet Center counselors across the country faced similar problems, and for the same good reasons. On the basis of its prior record, the VA merited the hostility.

Vietnam vets were completely isolated from their culture. The final irony was their isolation even from the mental health professionals employed by the one agency responsible for caring for "him who shall have borne the battle."

In small groups across the country where veterans had come together to help themselves, in a few organized rap groups in the early seventies, and finally, in the Vet Centers, the stories of alienation and isolation began to come out. For many, life no longer held any meaning or purpose. A succession of marriages and jobs, sleepless nights and depression, had been their lot for years. The future seemed equally bleak. "It don't mean nothin'" had become a pervasive attitude of mind.

RITES OF RE-ENTRY

All the talk in the early rap groups about parades, public welcomes, memorials, and the like were simply expressions of the vets' desire to return as full members of society. Indeed, parades and memorials are symbols of public recognition, even of absolution. Recognition, reentry, and cleansing are required by every warrior who returns from battle to rejoin his people.

Ancient tribes had rites of purification for returning warriors. It was understood in ancient times that a man performed acts in combat that were not permitted in his society. But the warrior acts on behalf of his people. The violence and savagery of combat, the atrocity, slaughter, rape, and pillaging that ordinarily accompany war, are unacceptable behavior in any society, but they are permitted in war, where they are done in the name of the society. Warriors required cleansing from these acts before they could regain their place among their people. In this way the tribe both distanced itself from the acts of its warriors and yet accepted responsibility for them. After the cleansing ritual, the warriors were readmitted to full and respected status.

The Vietnam warriors, like their ancient predecessors, were conscious of having performed in war acts unacceptable within their society. Like the fighting men of antiquity, they required a ritual of cleansing that entailed both a welcome home and the acceptance of some responsibility by the people for acts they had committed. But this was not to be, for we Americans view war much differently than did our ancient ancestors.

In America, the notion of cleansing has been lost from the rites of reentry, supplanted by the idea that the justice of our national cause renders all acts of war moral. Americans welcome home victorious crusaders, men who have fought for righteousness against an evil foe. No questions are asked about the war itself. The single exception in American history seems to be that of the defeated Confederate Army after the Civil War, but General Lee and his soldiers rode off into another type of mythology. The paradigmatic welcome Vietnam vets had in mind was that granted to the victorious crusaders of World War II.

To some extent, two National Salutes, the Vietnam Memorial in Washington, and the New York ticker-tape parade, have done much to narrow the gulf between the vets and the rest of society. It is significant, however, that these events were delayed by a full ten years and could be held only at a time when the images of the war had faded from public memory. Nowhere within the public welcome was the notion of cleansing to be found. Neither was there any idea of a moral connection between the American people and the combat actions of American soldiers.

Even more significant is that public recognition of Vietnam veterans coincided with a revival of the notion that the Vietnam War was a "noble cause." The "welcome home" of Vietnam veterans occurred during an era of rejoicing over the successful use of force in Grenada, tolerance for an unprecedented arms buildup, and increasing acceptance of the possibility of armed American intervention in Central America. Perhaps this is mere historical coincidence, but I think not. It seems that the welcome home could not have occurred before the American people had allowed the profoundly disturbing images of Vietnam to fade from memory. At the same time, they had finally begun to re-mythologize the warriors in classic American fashion.

For years, homebound America was forced to watch the reality of the war in Vietnam on the evening news. Television covered the Tet offensive and countless other battles. TV, newspapers, and the newsweeklies covered the disconcerting stories of returning veterans. The media uncovered the story of the My Lai massacre. The horror of Vietnam was for years a large part of American life.

PENETRATING THE FACADE

Long isolation produced people with exceptional talent for penetrating sham and facade. One vet I know claims to have a "bullshit detector that can pick up a cow's fart at ten miles." Men who went overseas as normal, gregarious teenagers spent hours in Vietnam silently stalking trails and waiting at ambush sites. There was ample time to think. Their reflection period was lengthened by the long isolation at home. For some this became creative solitude; for others it produced only pain. But however else they may have used the time of enforced isolation, most veterans I know have highly developed bullshit detectors.

Indeed, there is plenty of bullshit to detect. For example, the crass materialism of our society. Young men who cut their teeth on the products of the world's most advanced technology wondered why the peasant army opposing them was so good. The American love affair with money and material things somehow made less sense after Vietnam. The contrast between our way of life and that of the Vietnamese people is still a cause for some unease among vets. If God's favor is found in wealth and the gadgets of war it can produce, then who needs God's favor? The North Vietnamese did quite well without it.

When one has lived on the edge of death, it becomes possible to sort out from life's trivia what is truly important. A kind of culture shock developed for vets who returned home to find a society immersed in the pursuit of the insignificant. Once again, America had not changed, but they had. Others may take seriously the playthings we produce for our own pleasure, but after Vietnam the binges of a consumer society seem almost obscene.

For most vets, the primary locus of bullshit is still found in the public sector—the utterances of politicians, the promises of the VA, the policies and pronouncements of government.

A rap group—which sooner or later gets around to all these issues—may seem to an outsider like a repository of pure cynicism. Not only the war but every corner of American society takes a drubbing. What is really taking place during these sessions, however, is a search for deeper meaning. If the roots of religious faith are called into question as a result of the war, so, too, is every aspect of the culture in which that faith developed.

CHAPTER THREE: MARCHING ALONG TOGETHER AGAIN

The journey out of the Vietnam night began as a long march that became a national movement. For those who wish to isolate the religious and moral spheres from the realities and necessities of daily life, the journey seems at first to be most unspiritual. But if one believes, as I do, that the sacred pervades the secular, then marches and movements of all kinds are inseparable from the religious journey. Political and economic struggles bear directly upon emotional states, and all these relate to moral order. The religious sphere includes every corner of life but transcends them all as we travel individually and together toward God. The veterans' passage must be understood in these terms.

VETS AGAINST THE WAR

For some vets the personal journey started with a march on Washington to throw down in anger and disgust their combat medals. America watched on television as its newest veterans protested against the war they had fought. Others took their first steps out of darkness in a veterans' rap group in New York City. The war could be buried beneath consciousness for just so long.

In small numbers, tentatively at first, vets began to come out of the closet.

All across the country vets began to seek each other out. Self-help centers sprang up. Even within the VA some people began to listen as a few psychiatrists started to take war experiences seriously. Veterans in San Francisco, Santa Rosa, St. Louis, and other cities put together community-based programs to serve vets in need.

Shut off from real community with anyone else, veterans began to find one another. Even this was not easy, because the only people you could truly count on and trust completely were the men you really knew and loved—the ones who had been with you in combat, who had shared your little piece of jungle, lived your part of the nightmare. But most often these men couldn't be found. They were dead, or maybe they made it back but were living in different parts of the country. They had simply dropped out of sight. Vietnam vets had become loners, not sure they could trust anyone—even each other.

The war itself provided the first opportunity for banding together in some sort of concerted action. Opposition to the war during the presidential campaign of 1968 brought together some of the men who were later to form the Vietnam Veterans Against the War (VVAW). Both Republican and Democratic conventions were aware of their presence. Some who visited the conventions were treated to police brutality for what they had to say.

As opposition to the war grew, the VVAW played a significant role. It was very difficult for the American right wing to dismiss as mushy-headed liberals the veterans who marched against their own war. These men protested the war by throwing down their medals in disgust in front of the White House. The congressional hearings in 1971 provided another public forum for veterans who opposed the war.

Not many veterans were as eloquent as John Kerry, a former naval officer, now U.S. senator from Massachusetts who spoke to the Senate Foreign Relations Committee during the April 1971 gathering of Vietnam veterans in Washington. Kerry said:

"We wish that a merciful God could wipe away our own memories of that service as easily as this administration has wiped away their memory of us. But all they have done and all they can do by this denial is to make more clear than ever our own determination to undertake one last mission—to search out and destroy the last vestige of this barbaric war, to pacify our own hearts, to conquer the hate and fear that have driven this country these last ten years and more, so when thirty years from now our brothers go down the street without a leg, without an arm, or a face and small boys ask why, we will be able to say "Vietnam" and not mean a desert, not a filthy obscene memory, but mean instead the place where America turned and where soldiers like us helped in the turning."[23]

Whatever individual and isolated veterans may have thought about the activities of the VVAW and those who publicly opposed the war, their success demonstrated that concerted action was not only possible but effective. The war and the attempt to end it had provided the first opportunity for a common effort.

RAP GROUPS: HEALING AT LAST

The first item on almost every veteran's agenda was inner healing, but it was abundantly clear that the psychic and spiritual wounds of war were only deepened by isolation. Healing and the restoration of inner peace demanded another common effort.

Veterans almost instinctively began to come together and form rap groups. These were easy and informal sessions in which men could gather to talk about the war. Eventually the rap groups were to become the primary source of healing for people who were really hurting. They also became a major instrument through which the Vietnam veterans movement achieved most of its goals.

Robert Jay Lifton is a psychiatrist and researcher internationally known for his work with survivors of the atomic bombing at Hiroshima and victims of the Nazi holocaust. Unlike most psychiatrists in the early seventies, he took the veterans seriously. He and Chaim Shatan, another psychiatrist sensitive to the veterans, worked with rap groups in the New York-New Haven area. Lifton writes:

> The veterans' rap groups came into being because the veterans sensed that they had more psychological work to do in connection with the war. It is important to emphasize that the veterans themselves initiated the groups. The men knew that they were "hurting," but did not want to seek help from the Veterans Administration, which they associated with the military, the target of much of their rage. And though they were in psychological pain, they did not consider themselves patients. They wanted to understand what they had been through, begin to heal themselves, and at the same time make known to the American public the human costs of the war.[24]

Lifton also understood that the veterans had two aspirations: "healing themselves while finding a mode of political expression."[25] These two goals were actually inseparable. Without some form of political-social expression there could be no healing of the psychic wounds of war.

Shad Meshad, a social worker who served a tour in Vietnam with the Army as a psychology officer, talked in the early seventies of the "circle of treatment." At that time Meshad was in charge of a Vietnam veterans ward at Brentwood VA Hospital in West Los Angeles. He realized that intra psychic healing was impossible apart from a total "resocialization" back into the community. For Meshad this entailed veterans telling their stories publicly and having some political impact on the society that sent them to war. It also meant that the veteran must have a real job, not just a minimum wage or "make work" form of employment. The veteran must once again interact with his society as a mature and respected citizen. He must have a place in his local community and a respected position in the nation. Meshad's notion of the circle of treatment later came to include VA mental health services taken into the community.

Like John Kerry, Lifton, Shatan, and Meshad understood very early that the wounds of war demanded political, economic, and spiritual reintegration of the veterans into society. Without a total re-socialization there could be no genuine healing. This insight resulted from a profound and accurate reading of what the veterans were saying—virtually from the first moment of their return from combat. It is an intuition that pervades the Vietnam veterans movement.

The overarching vision is one of total healing by way of a new and deeper reintegration of the individual veteran into society. But this healing can never be a one-way street. Society must now open itself to the vets and their message. The people who sent them overseas must now accept the full consequences of their return.

Individual vets sought relief from the adverse psychological effects resulting from combat—depression, sleep disorders, flashbacks, etc., but I never met a veteran who was willing to relinquish the insights or the altered vision of the world that grew out of his Vietnam experience. The burden of this new worldview is that it must be shared. Returning vets felt that they should exert a profound impact on society. They still believe this. They remain convinced that the American people must allow themselves to be changed by the experiences of their sons and daughters in Vietnam. In the lexicon of Vietnam veterans, re-socialization or reintegration always means this kind of reciprocal relationship with society. Veterans are both unable and unwilling to sneak back into their homeland and resume life as if Vietnam never happened.

LOS ANGELES: A MICROCOSM

The common effort presaged by the VVAW—then given different shape in the first rap groups and self-help centers—began to accelerate in the early seventies. I am personally familiar with what happened during this period in Los Angeles; I later learned that our experience there was fairly typical. In recounting the Los Angeles story, I intend only to sketch an outline in microcosm of what occurred at about the same time throughout the entire country. The specific events and details, of course, differ from place to place, but the aims, goals, and means chosen to achieve our ends were remarkably similar across the land.

The journey out of the Vietnam night began with a desire for total healing. Given society's attitude toward the vets at the time, it was abundantly clear that one's only comrades on the journey would be other vets. In Los Angeles several efforts had begun in different parts of the city, independently and in isolation from each other. By 1973 we began to reach out to each other, to meet, talk, plan, share, our experiences and devise common goals and strategies.

The Brentwood VA Hospital had established a Vietnam veterans inpatient ward. Brentwood was one of two large VA hospitals in West Los Angeles. Its function was to provide mental health treatment, while its companion facility, Wadsworth, provided medical treatment. Brentwood Director, John Valance, and Social Work Chief, John Fulton, both sympathetic to

Vietnam veterans, had hired Shad Meshad, a Vietnam vet and clinical social worker with neither Ph.D. nor M.D. degree, to run the Vietnam veterans ward. Most of the people hired to assist him were also veterans with counseling or social work training.

In every hospital situation I have encountered, the "doctor" calls all the shots, but this was not the case in the Brentwood Viet-vet ward. Individual therapy and rap sessions were geared toward dealing specifically with the psychological issues resulting from combat. Psychiatrists and clinical psychologists who could not adjust to this new and different approach to therapy were simply thrown off the ward by Meshad. Many on the psychiatry and psychology staffs were not happy with the arrangement, but Valance and Fulton continued to back Meshad and support the Viet-vet effort. The Vietnam therapists soon began seeing people on an outpatient basis, as well. In this, the situation in Los Angeles differed from that in many areas. There was a place where veterans could go that offered legitimate and effective therapy. Most Brentwood psychiatrists I met during this period had not the slightest clue as to how to deal with Vietnam veterans, but at least I could refer my clients who needed treatment to Meshad's ward in the basement of the hospital.

One lesson we learned in Los Angeles was not to take traditional mental health services too seriously. Psychiatrists and clinical psychologists could function within their well-defined parameters, but they didn't know how to treat combat-related stress. Nor could they give any guidance on how to achieve the kind of total reintegration into society that we knew was necessary. The result was that some of us began doing the same kind of things that were being done on the Viet-vet ward. We still referred the more serious cases to Meshad's people, but we began to do much on our own. The Brentwood ward taught us that there was no mystique involved in healing the wounds of war. We took the combat experience seriously and worked through the grief, rage, and depression with other veterans. We certainly didn't wait for the experts to show us how to do it. In fact, it wasn't long before we began teaching the experts.

Another institution arose out of need in Los Angeles in the early seventies: the Center for Veterans Rights, an organization formed to obtain upgraded discharges for veterans. A great number of veterans had received other than honorable discharges after their Vietnam service. Sometimes these discharges resulted from court-martial convictions, but often they were administrative discharges "for the good of the service." Like much else that occurred in the cynical and morally corrupt environment of Vietnam, these discharges, often unjust and inappropriate, were given at the whim of the commander. The consequences of any discharge other than an honorable one were severe. One's future employment and career plans were jeopardized by "bad paper."

I remember a battalion commander in Vietnam who had in his unit a man hopelessly addicted to heroin. The soldier, a black, had committed no serious offenses, having earned only a few Article 15s (non-judicial punishment for minor offenses). He had gone through a period of detoxification, "cold turkey," in Long Binh Jail. The man was due to end his tour and his military service in about two weeks, and the commanding officer had called me in to discuss the disposition of his case. The colonel was determined to give him an administrative "other than honorable discharge" because of his heroin problem. I argued that there was no reason to do this. The man had been through his tour without committing any serious offense. What he needed, I argued, was treatment for his addiction through VA programs. There was no reason to saddle him with bad paper that would hamper his future efforts at finding employment. The colonel pounded his desk and shouted, "Goddam it, Chaplain, the New Testament talks about justice." I stood up, went over to his desk, pounded it, and shouted: "Goddam it, Colonel, the New Testament talks about mercy." The colonel, a churchgoing man, relented and let the man go home. Unfortunately, there were many officers who shared the colonel's propensity for giving administrative discharges, of which blacks and Hispanics received a disproportionately large number.

The Center for Veterans Rights had begun as a project of the Los Angeles County Department of Military and Veterans Affairs, but it soon became an independent operation, headed by a veteran named Pat Wood, who later became a lawyer. For years it was located on the property of St. John's Episcopal Church in Los Angeles. Wood and his counselors became experts in military law, and they were real tigers when it came to pushing the military to upgrade discharges and the VA to grant veterans benefits to vets with bad paper. VA rating boards and adjudicators tended to withhold benefits whenever possible for vets with bad paper. VA regulations concerning the benefits available for each kind of discharge were labyrinthine, but Pat Wood, his successor, Jerry Melnyk, and their associates gave the rating boards a battle in each case.

The military boards of discharge review in Washington and the boards they occasionally sent West to sit in Los Angeles became aware that the center was around. Its work resulted in a great many upgraded discharges. Many veterans acquired new hope and a new beginning in life because of these dedicated and committed people.

The problem of bad paper is a national one. There were—and still are—a number of organizations across the country that perform the same function as the Center for Veterans Rights in Los Angeles. For countless veterans they have made the difference between living a jobless existence on the streets and having a decent life. Here again, the lesson was learned: an evil outcome of the war must be confronted. Don't wait for the government, the experts, or the benevolence of the American people. Band together and act to get the job done.

The groups that came together and brought into being the Vietnam veterans movement soon learned that local political machinery had to be influenced. Faced with the general public's virtual amnesia regarding the existence of Vietnam veterans, there was no alternative but to exert pressure on government at all levels to secure benefits of any kind. Every minority group has learned this lesson. Vietnam veterans were no exception.

In Los Angeles, Robert L. Kingsbury, a retired Army major and director of the county Department of Military and Veterans Affairs, devised the notion of a county commission that would report directly to the Board of Supervisors on Vietnam veterans issues. For those not familiar with the California political system, each of the fifty-eight counties is headed by a five-person board with both executive and legislative authority. These boards are tremendously powerful. In 1974, when the Vietnam Veterans Advisory Commission was formed, Los Angeles County had a larger budget than forty-two of the fifty states. The supervisors were all male and were referred to as "the five kings." By this time the politicians in Los Angeles knew there was some sort of problem and a potential for quite a bit of trouble from Vietnam veterans, so they accepted Kingsbury's idea. The commission was established for the specific purpose of exerting political pressure on federal and state governments through the supervisors' lobby in Washington and Sacramento. The commission was also to submit recommendations on county veterans issues to the supervisors for their direct vote.

Each supervisor appointed two veterans to the commission. Robert Leong, a former captain in Special Forces, with two tours in Vietnam, was the first chairman. Leong at the time was a student at UCLA. The county commission provided the first taste of real political power for Vietnam vets in Los Angeles.

The commission held hearings, submitted recommendations to the board, and indeed acquired a voice in Sacramento and in Washington.

During the mid-seventies, Los Angeles Mayor Tom Bradley established a committee of Vietnam veterans to advise him on significant issues. Through the committee (which selected Bob Leong, now very skilled as a political leader, as its first chairman), Mayor Bradley was able to obtain jobs for veterans in both the private and the public sector. He also lent his support to our efforts to end the TV and movie stereotyping of Vietnam vets as kill-crazed and emotionally disturbed people.

Another significant organization in Los Angeles was a self-help center established by Ken Brooks, a veteran who served in the military between the Korean and Vietnam wars. Located in south central Los Angeles, the Veterans Counseling and Guidance Center served a predominantly black veteran clientele, assisting them in obtaining VA benefits and jobs and working through the impact of the war.

Community-based programs with veterans components were also established in the largely Hispanic East Los Angeles area and in other parts of the black community.

My own role at this time was "community service specialist" at the VA Regional Office. My function was to provide social work services to veterans who came into the office or called in. I did some of everything: psychological counseling, job finding, acting as ombudsman within the agency, locating housing for veterans, and some community organizing. I spent at least half my time out of the office, with the veterans, wherever they happened to be.

By this time, many of the VA Regional Office employees were Vietnam veterans themselves. They clearly understood and were sympathetic to the issues. Their impact began to be felt throughout the agency. The director and several key supervisors were willing to listen to their subordinates, becoming more informed and responsive to the needs of Vietnam vets. This resulted in a great deal of tension within the agency between the younger Vietnam vet employees, who dealt face-to-face with the clients, and the more experienced people—the senior claims adjudicators and rating-board specialists—who seldom saw the clients. Slowly and painfully, even the VA itself began to change.

It became increasingly clear that we all had to work together if we were to accomplish anything. The isolation to which Vietnam veterans had become accustomed only kept them from effective action on their own behalf. We began to surmount the natural suspicions and antagonisms held by people of different ethnic and racial groups. We started to close the gap between people who worked for the VA and those whose jobs were to battle the agency. We began to rely on each other's skills and expertise, referring veterans to the appropriate group for help.

The Vietnam veteran community in Los Angeles never remotely resembled a close-knit group of friends, but we committed ourselves to transcending our own limitations and interests. In the process, we acquired a profound respect for each other, and, of course, some very deep friendships developed. Most important, the large veteran population of Los Angeles was well served.

Of course, once in a while we got in each other's way while fighting for a slice of the pie. Bad feelings sometimes resulted. On one occasion, a veteran who was known to carry a weapon was asked to testify before the county commission. One member of the commission harbored a deep-seated dislike of the man who was to testify. Bob Leong, the chairman, made it clear before the meeting that he would tolerate no nonsense and that proceedings were to be conducted in a businesslike manner. The meeting went surprisingly well. I walked out afterward with the chairman and the commission member who disliked the principal witness. The latter confessed that he was glad that so-and-so remained cool and didn't go for his weapon. Bob and I sincerely agreed with him. "But," he said, "I was ready for him." He then reached into his boot and pulled out a small caliber pistol. A shoot-out at the county commission meeting never occurred, but it could have. In Los Angeles, as elsewhere, men trained and experienced in violence could have—but usually did not—resort to violence. The journey out of the night demanded that violence be laid aside—but there were some close calls along the way.

In Los Angeles, as elsewhere throughout the country, thousands of veterans were working their way through the psychic scars of war, finding jobs, having discharges upgraded, and obtaining VA benefits. Inner healing and reestablishing links with society had begun to take place. Locally, informally, and in a very loose fashion, a ground-swell was under way. Veterans were breaking out of their isolation, out of the night.

COMING TOGETHER AT LAST

On a national level, symposia and seminars were put together to deal with veterans' issues. Often these were sponsored by universities, and they brought together knowledgeable and interested people from different areas of the country. Arthur Eggendorf, a former Vietnam soldier, Charles Figley, a Marine Corps veteran, and John Wilson, a conscientious objector during the war, all Ph.D. psychologists, began doing serious research on the impact of the war on veterans. Their findings became known at the seminars and symposia. All three have subsequently continued their work and published widely. Other clinicians and researchers began serious work with veterans.

In the political arena, a very determined group of veterans under the leadership of Robert 0. Muller, a former Marine Corps officer who had become a paraplegic as a result of his

Vietnam service, put together a national organization, the Vietnam Veterans of America (VVA). The VVA exercises increasing influence and political clout. It has never fit the mold of a traditional veterans organization. Its relationship with other veterans groups, with the VA, and especially with whatever administration happens to be in power has often been strained. In this it reflects the attitudes of its national constituency. Without such an organization, Vietnam veterans would not have achieved many of their goals.

Veterans began to take heart because some former soldiers and marines—and a few journalists who had covered the war—began to tell their story in book form. Biographical works, histories, and novels captured the interest of the public.

In January 1977, President Jimmy Carter took office and appointed Max Cleland to head the Veterans Administration. Cleland had served with the Army and was severely injured in combat: he lost both legs and one arm. After his release from the hospital, Max Cleland had testified before the Senate Veterans Affairs Committee. In his testimony he had likened the psychological impact of the war to "a series of secondary explosions" in his head. Alan Cranston, senator from California and chairman of the committee, had been impressed with Cleland and supported his views.

With Max Cleland as administrator, the Veterans Administration could no longer evade its responsibility to provide adequate psychological treatment for Vietnam veterans. Different models of treatment had been suggested for years, but the VA medical system was unwilling to depart from the standard medical model of psychiatric treatment. Max Cleland insisted that they devise a new approach.

In October 1977, Shad Meshad, who had by then acquired a national reputation, and Chuck Figley, whose research was nationally known and respected, were called to the VA Central Office to discuss the specifics of a program. I was also invited to take part in the effort. We were asked to "put together a program."

On Halloween night and into the morning hours of the next day, Shad and I put on paper the ideas that had evolved from the work in his Vietnam veterans unit, from Chuck Figley's research, from the collective experience of all of us in Los Angeles, and from anything else we knew of that seemed to work anywhere in the country. We finished our final draft about eight in the morning and immediately presented the document to Guy McMichael, the VA's chief lawyer. He liked it and submitted it to Max Cleland and other officials within the agency.

The VA established a committee to refine our program design in light of the best knowledge and experience then available. Committee membership consisted of veterans, clinicians, and specialists from around the country. Shad Meshad was a member of the group. Early in 1979, the VA submitted the program to the administration and to Congress as a legislative proposal. Congress (with powerful assistance from Senator Cranston and the senate committee) passed the bill in June, and the Vietnam Veterans Readjustment Counseling Program—the Vet Centers—was born.

In a parallel development, the Disabled American Veterans, a national service organization with considerable political influence and collective common sense, established an outreach program to work with Vietnam veterans. Service officers (experts in VA claims who argue cases before rating boards) were sent out into the community in a special effort to reach Vietnam veterans. These men were expected to do individual counseling with veterans. Service-officer training was based on the research of Dr. John Wilson. The Disabled American Veterans made a real commitment to work as seriously in behalf of Vietnam veterans as they had for veterans of other wars.

By the end of the 1970s, local, regional, and national efforts had begun to coalesce and bring some tangible results. The journey out of darkness, loneliness, and despair was far more than just therapy and individual counseling for the thousands of vets who still bore the scars of war. The journey had taken on the characteristics of a real social movement. People had started listening to the veterans; Vietnam books appeared on the market, the political movement was taken seriously, and a national program of readjustment counseling had finally passed through Congress. A reciprocal relationship with society—real give-and-take had begun.

VET CENTERS AND SURVIVAL TACTICS

The first of the "store front" Vet Centers opened late in 1979, almost five years after the fall of Saigon. The VA program was at last under way. By then the majority of veterans had been out of combat from eight to fifteen years. They trickled into the centers at first; then the numbers became a steady flow. More recently, the influx of veterans into the centers has come to resemble a torrent. At the time of this writing, there are 189 Vet Centers nationwide.

Vet Centers are places of genuine healing. They have become the spiritual centers of the Vietnam veteran's movement. Depression, rage, guilt, and repressed grief are the terrible burdens of the Vietnam veteran. Only when these are lifted is it possible to resume the business of living. In Vet Centers across the country, burdens shared become burdens lifted, and life begins anew.

The first thing that happens in a Vet Center is the formation of real community. Men whose last significant attempt at human contact was aborted by a spit in the face—or by one of rejection's more subtle forms—take the risk again. At first it is with fellow vets and counselors, then with wives, girlfriends, and finally, with the society "out there."

A veteran community forms around a Vet Center. Its style

and ethos resemble the camaraderie of the combat zone. Commitment, genuine concern, and affection for each other are hallmarks of one's newfound "unit." The mission of the Vet Center community is to make the final psychological DEROS from Vietnam. The objective of this last campaign of the Vietnam War is to help people become functional in the fullest sense "back in the world." It is no accident that the person in charge of the Vet Center is officially titled the "team leader."

Obstacles in the way of complete DEROS might be drug or alcohol addiction. If this is the case, the team devises tactics to defeat the enemy. Some tactics always employed are individual counseling, combat-vet rap groups, marriage counseling, and groups for spouses.

Most often other tactics are required, as well. In San Diego, for example, a number of the men found they were addicted to both drugs and alcohol in addition to being addicted to the painful combat memories of Vietnam. They formed the Triple Threat Group. Based on the principles of Alcoholics Anonymous, this group confronts the triple threat: drugs, alcohol, and Vietnam. Triple-threat recovery is, in the words of one of the group members, a "heavy-duty operation." It has been very successful.

A VET WHO SURVIVED

One of the men who made it through triple-threat recovery is Randy Way.

Drafted in 1968, Randy found himself with the Fourth Infantry Division near Pleiku. He saw quite a bit of heavy combat with his unit and was wounded "on April Fool's Day, 1969." His perception of the war is succinct: "Except for the guys, what I saw goin' on was bullshit." A veteran of many firefights, he was particularly bothered by the guerrilla aspects of the war—being shot at by an unseen enemy. "If I know what I've got to deal with, I can do it, but if I can't see it, fuck it."

A Vietnam soldier at the age of twenty, he had an acquaintance with drugs that was usual among teenagers of the time. He had used pot but was afraid of hard drugs because he had seen its effects on some of his friends. In Vietnam he began smoking pot again; he smoked in the field—sometimes with officers as well as with other enlisted men. After he was wounded, a soldier from New York invited him to try opium. He refused until the man pointed to his M-16 and to the opium apparatus and said, "You're not afraid of this gun, why be afraid of this one?" It seemed to make sense, so he tried it.

After he was "turned on" to opium, "nothing mattered." "I could walk through Pleiku like I owned it." Here at last was release from heavy combat and the bullshit of Vietnam. He used opium about a dozen times while in Vietnam, mixing it with pot and "number-ten downers."

When he got back to his home in San Diego in June 1969, his father (a retired Marine "lifer") took one look at him and could only say: "Oh, shit." Randy married a sixteen-year-old girl, and they soon had a son. The marriage broke up after three years. For a time Randy had custody of his son, but he lost that after a court battle.

Life became progressively worse, and his dope habit grew. Before long he was supporting a very heavy heroin habit. He reports that for about six years he was a "hardcore heroin user." He went through periods when he had to have a weapon; then he would reach the point where he couldn't stand to be around one. But finally he became a "paranoid dope fiend" and carried a twelve-gauge shot-gun, even sleeping with it.

A turning point came when he decided to measure the shotgun to see if he could put the barrel in his mouth and pull the trigger with his toes, "like they do in the movies." He realized then that something was wrong. He asked himself if he had lived this long, surviving Vietnam, to end up killing himself. He decided to seek help and entered a hospital inpatient program for drug addicts.

While hospitalized, he was contacted by another veteran who had successfully completed the same program. The vet visited Randy every day and convinced him to come to the Vet Center rap group. At this point he decided to be a survivor rather than a victim. So I'm a Vietnam vet and a drug addict, so what!" He became a regular at the rap group and an integral part of the veteran community. With two other vets who saw the connection between Vietnam and addiction, he founded the Triple Threat Group.

About three weeks after coming to his first rap-group session, Randy, who owns and operates a scaffold company, was working on the chapel tower of a convent of Roman Catholic Benedictine sisters. He knew they were watching him, so he performed some daredevil antics. When he finished the job, Sister Paula Thompson, the superior, told him that they were praying for him not to fall or hurt himself. He was impressed with this and spent about ten minutes talking with her. At the end of the conversation, he asked if she could teach him to pray again, because "I've got nothing in me anymore." A former altar boy in the Lutheran church, he, like so many veterans, had nothing to do with religion after Vietnam. He met with Sister Paula about once a week and still sees her on a regular basis. He believes that a spiritual program is essential for healing the wounds of war as well as recovery from drug addiction: "Anyone who believes you can do it all yourself is full of shit."

POLITICAL TACTICS

All kinds of tactics are appropriate to achieve the goal of full recovery. At one point in San Diego it seemed that no one outside the Vietnam veteran group was responding to any of our needs. Some vets had been complaining of insensitive treatment by doctors at the VA Hospital, and we had a string of hard luck in finding jobs for vets. Things just weren't going well. Toward the end of a Tuesday evening rap group, somebody decided that it was time to take some action. Somebody suggested a squad-sized operation against the VA hospital—just a little bit of damage to the property to attract their attention. Cooler heads prevailed, and a different tactic was selected. We decided to try to change the system politically, so we formed a political group on the spot that evening, the Vietnam Veterans of San Diego (VVSD). Jack Lyon, a former Marine captain, platoon leader in Vietnam, and silver-star winner, was elected president of the organization. Lyon proved to be a remarkably competent and inspiring leader who gave direction to the local movement and ensured the success of the projects we undertook in San Diego.

The first real mission of the VVSD came shortly after its inception. Pete Wilson, then mayor of San Diego, now U.S. senator from California, wanted to do something symbolic to honor Vietnam vets. Someone on his staff suggested a tree planting and speech with media coverage at the Veterans Memorial Building in San Diego's Balboa Park. The word went back that planting trees and making speeches was largely "bullshit." We would cooperate, however, if Mayor Wilson would actually do something about getting jobs for Vietnam veterans. Mayor Wilson agreed. He did plant his tree and make his speech, but he also publicly committed himself to work for jobs for vets. He proved to be as good as his word. The mayor ordered his staff to set up a liaison with a consortium of public and private employers and to get the jobs. Whenever city staff seemed to falter in their efforts, Jack Lyon successfully brought pressure to bear. Several hundred jobs for vets resulted.

Another mission the VVSD undertook was to fund and set up a halfway house for drug-addicted veterans. Randy Way, who became the second president of VVSD, played a crucial role in the project. After several years of fund-raising, the dream was realized. It was a proud and happy moment when the Landing Zone opened in downtown San Diego in late 1984 with forty-six beds available. Every bed was soon occupied. The Landing Zone is always full and has a waiting list.

A SPIRITUALITY FOR THE JOURNEY

Three deeply ingrained characteristics of the American soul also died for the soldiers in the jungles of Vietnam. Innocence, exuberance, and the American "can do" feeling—qualities that usually accompany religion in America—are no longer possible for veterans of Southeast Asian combat.

Most people, of course, sooner or later lose the moral innocence of youth. The death of loved ones, illness, and the evils of the world impinge upon everyone who lives long enough. Combat and atrocity, however, alter the very context within which thoughts and feelings arise. Firsthand experience with evil of this magnitude changes profoundly the way in which one views the world.

Combat veterans and the victims of every war know this, as do survivors of the holocaust and other genocides. Those who confront mass starvation, systematic apartheid, and grinding destitution also understand life in a significantly different way.

Whatever their own personal experience may be, however, Americans enjoy another kind of collective and national innocence. An underlying, unspoken, and unquestioned assumption within our culture is that we are the morally innocent agents of good in an evil world. This is not something we are taught in any formal sense. It "is not a matter of idea or concept or doctrine; rather, it is a part of the texture of growing up in the United States."[26] Vietnam veterans lost both their personal and their cultural innocence.

What lay beyond innocence? For a long time, nothing. During the years of isolation and exclusion from society, the only fruits of Vietnam were bitterness and loneliness. The first bursts of energy to be released within the veteran groups were eruptions from the deepest levels of consciousness and feeling. A new insight was born within these small communities. Vets became aware for the first time that beyond lost innocence and shattered faith, beyond bitterness and despair, beyond even war and atrocity, there is life, healing, and hope.

The typical American exuberance—which almost always accompanies religion—enriches our national culture, to be sure. But we demand exuberance as a constant feature of life. This is really an indication of cultural and religious adolescence. It is almost a national sin not to "have a nice day." Vietnam veterans endured days lengthening into years that were not at all nice. But the vets found that beyond exuberance lies a deeper well-spring of human healing power. The veterans who spoke against the war revealed the depth of their own anguish and turmoil. Yet they were convinced they could end the war and help heal society. Rap groups and self-help centers would have been impossible apart from the profound conviction that veterans could heal each other and in the process transform themselves and even change society. The Vet Centers came into being only because a handful of people believed that the bitter ashes of despair could be transformed into personal healing for hundreds of thousands of veterans.

Americans are a "can do" people. Since our first conquest of the wilderness during the colonial period and from the glorious days of the political experiment that created a nation, we have encountered nothing we could not accomplish. Military might has often been the means selected to accomplish national goals; it had never failed us—until Vietnam. Vietnam represented a historic failure in the use of power, an event for which we were totally unprepared. Military failure is simply unacceptable to Americans.

Relegating veterans to the role of moral pariahs probably had as much to do with the fall of South Vietnam to the Communists as with any real revulsion on the part of Americans to the killing, that took place there. As much scapegoats for being unsuccessful agents of American power as for being killers in combat, veterans were forced to bear in isolation the burden of failure. Stripped of self respect, Vietnam veterans were reduced to social, moral, and political impotence. They had supposed it was their turn to walk in the shoes of heroes, to show the power of innocence in the face of evil. When that didn't work out, they found that a fall from power was also a fall from grace. They became the powerless.

Like the loss of innocence and the death of exuberance, the fall from power had a profound impact on the veterans. Denied access to society, they became, in a social and moral sense, what many of them had become physically in Vietnam-survivors. Survivors can function without most of the trappings and even some of the necessities of life. Veterans "back in the world" simply learned to get along without many of the cultural and emotional props most Americans need. Here the experience in Vietnam, especially their acquaintance with the enemy, definitely helped. A guerrilla soldier has very little in the way of any kind of comfort, but he survives and sometimes even thrives. Comparatively powerless with respect to the overwhelming might of the greatest military machine on earth, the guerrilla soldiers on the other side did quite well. That lesson has never been lost on Vietnam veterans.

The now powerless vets had no choice but to reach deeply into their own inner resources and to discover an untapped reserve. Most people, carried along by the prevailing cultural currents, are never compelled to go that deeply into themselves. The veterans' journey out of the night began with a journey inward and with the discovery of grace beyond innocence, hope beyond exuberance, and power at the very heart of failure.

I do not intend to idealize or to generalize the Vietnam veterans' struggle. The story, after all, is really hundreds of thousands of individual stories. Some personal chronicles end in suicide, insanity, or tragic failure. Others are inspiring by any standards. Most are quite ordinary. But there is a common thread in the stories: Vietnam and its impact overcome through a common effort. I have attempted to interpret in this chapter only the primordial impulses that brought healing to Vietnam veterans and that propelled them from bitter isolation into a powerful national force.

Despite the advances made by the Vietnam veterans movement—the Vet Centers, the national recognition, and the increasing acceptance by the American people—combat vets continue to suffer. A 1985 American Legion study showed that veterans who took part in heavy combat earn less annually than those with the same education who served elsewhere. The same study showed that combat vets have a higher divorce rate and suffer more unhappiness than their non-combat counterparts. Because the study was conducted among veterans who had been "resocialized sufficiently" to join the American Legion, there is good reason to think that the problems among other vets are even worse. The findings represent the "tip of the iceberg, or best case result."

The suffering is still there, but real progress has been made. It is still too soon to judge the impact upon veterans of "the Wall" in Washington, two "national salutes," belated parades, and the tenth-anniversary catharsis. Some vets feel they are now being lionized by a generation too young to remember Vietnam. Many are quite content to accept the role of noble warrior and to assume what they consider to be their rightful place among the nation's mythic heroes. Others fear they have been mythologized into noble warriors by a nation only too ready to forget Vietnam and willing to plunge its young sons and daughters once again into combat—this time in Central America.

At this time we can only speculate as to what impact these new currents will have on veterans and on America. Deep memories endure, however, and experience such as war, which alters consciousness, remains indelibly imprinted on the soul. What is primordial cannot be dislodged even by massive bombardments of the trivial and the banal. This leads me to believe that the original meaning ascribed to the Vietnam War by soldiers in the field, a meaning reinforced by the bitter homecoming, will endure despite all efforts to re-impose a more congenial interpretation. Even as it now reaches out to them in a tardy embrace, America will, I suspect, have continuing difficulty living with its Vietnam veterans. The impulse to change society, articulated by Kerry, remains a powerful one among veterans.

Even as they reached beyond the broken pieces of their lives, uncovering a reservoir of personal inner strength and power, the vets discovered a final paradox. Nothing is more deeply ingrained in our cultural tradition than the notion that the individual is supreme. The strong man copes on his own; he is independent and self-reliant. The soldier more than any other incarnates this strain of American individualism. But in recovering their personal psychic and spiritual resources, the veterans discovered the paradox that these personal resources are best employed not in a splendid display of individualism but rather in community.

Nothing is more in evidence at any gathering of Vietnam veterans than a deep, though often rough-hewn, sense of community. I was present at all the meetings that pulled together veterans from around the country to implement the VA outreach program. I have participated in many seminars, training sessions, and veterans gatherings since I left the Vet Center program. I am always inspired and moved by this profound sense of community. The motto of the first "National Salute" in 1982 expresses the new spiritual dynamic: "marching along together again."

CHAPTER FOUR: HEALING

"You won't believe this," he whispered, "but I'm afraid we're going to have a rocket attack." He knew in his mind, of course, that there was no danger of a rocket attack in Los Angeles. He himself had not experienced incoming rockets for at least eight years, but he still lived in his past—the Vietnam past.

He was in his late twenties; his face was covered with sweat. His muscles were tense, and fear was in his eyes. He looked out the window, his gaze resting on the golden arches in front of the McDonald's restaurant where we had been talking over coffee. He watched the endless stream of traffic on one of the busiest Streets in the San Fernando Valley. "I know you think I'm crazy," he continued, "but I've lived with this fear ever since Vietnam, and sometimes it overpowers me."

I asked him to watch the signal light at the intersection and to concentrate on the traffic. He began to immerse himself in the present moment, to become completely aware of his surroundings in Los Angeles, as once he had been "a hundred and fifty percent alert" in his environment in the Central Highlands of Vietnam.

As the minutes passed, his "gut" came into sync with his head. After the fear subsided, he was once again able to resume the conversation.

It was November 1979. The first Vet Center in the United States had opened only days before, but the office space was not yet ready for occupancy, so we used fast-food restaurants, bars, homes, streets, and parks as our offices. The veteran with whom I had sat over coffee was one of several hundred thousand who suffered from "a delayed stress reaction" to the Vietnam war.

DELAYED STRESS

Delayed stress is not a mental illness; it *is a reaction to the extreme stress* people experienced during and after the war in Southeast Asia. Psychiatrists and psychologists learned, largely because of their work with Vietnam veterans, that any kind of stressful experience can produce an emotional reaction that shows up only later. The death of a loved one, rape, fire, physical assault, and other traumatic events can cause a severe delayed reaction.

Vietnam stress reaction is delayed rather than experienced immediately because a soldier cannot allow himself to be emotionally overcome in combat. Men watched their closest friends die before their eyes but were unable to permit themselves to feel any grief or sorrow. As we saw earlier, the only emotions permissible in combat are those that contribute to survival. Every other feeling must be suppressed at once. To put it very bluntly, fear, grief, sorrow, and revulsion distract one from the business of killing. If one is an infantryman, killing is necessary to ensure one's own survival in a combat zone.

A soldier who takes the time or expends the energy to grieve for a buddy whose head has just been blown apart during a firefight invites his own death. Grieving after the battle is over is also impossible if a man knows that he will probably face the same kind of horror again at any moment. Survival requires the absorption of all one's personal resources. The only thing that kept a man alive until DEROS was rage channeled into combat action.

Fear, grief, sorrow, revulsion, and rage are indeed the emotional responses appropriate to combat. They are responses that endure for a lifetime—as long as memory lasts. But no set of emotions as powerful as those evoked by combat can remain permanently suppressed in the psyche. There must be a process of "working through" the feelings, of integrating them—and the combat memories—into the rest of one's life. "Vietnam," as someone so eloquently remarked, "remains freeze-dried in the eyes." It also remains bound up in the depths of the soul.

The normal emotional process by which most of us work through our reactions to the horrors of life was short-circuited for Vietnam veterans. Veterans of all wars have experienced the same emotional numbing in combat, but Vietnam was unique in a number of ways. I once heard John Wilson say that if the government had deliberately designed a program to induce madness in people, it could scarcely have improved on what it actually did to those who served in Vietnam. Here's what happened to most:

They went overseas alone—not by units but as individual passengers in a plane. They were sent to units already in the field as "newbies" and "FNGs" (fuckin' new guys). By the time they had become experienced in combat and established close bonds, they began to lose their friends, not just through death and wounds but because others were going home through DEROS. The war itself was largely a guerrilla action; there were no front lines, few pitched battles. Villagers sheltered an enemy cadre that was largely indistinguishable from the civilian population. Progress was measured not by territory gained but by an elusive and deceptive body count. Halfway through the tour in Vietnam there was a week away from warfare in the surreal world of Hong Kong, Sydney, or Honolulu—surreal because one had to return again to the realities of combat in the bush. At DEROS, a man was pulled out of the field, taken away from his friends, and sent home—only hours away from combat—irrevocably changed, to people who could no longer understand him and wouldn't listen to what he wanted to say. There was no possibility for most people to work through the overwhelming emotional reactions that now dominated their lives. "Delayed stress" is not nearly a strong enough term for the emotional suffering endured by countless veterans.

The contrast with World War II is striking. In that conflict, men went into combat as members of a unit. There was no mystical DEROS date against which survival was measured; they were in for the duration. Combat was, for the most part, action against large enemy units that were clearly distinguishable from the civilian population. Progress was measured by territory taken and held. Entire units were pulled back for occasional relief from battle, but there was no individual R and R in a different part of the world. When the war was over, soldiers returned together on troop ships. The process of working through the emotional scars of war began for many World War II veterans on the journey home, and with the men who had been with them in combat. Upon arrival, these veterans were greeted as heroes by an understanding and grateful people.

Not surprisingly, returned veterans of the Vietnam War often exhibit certain "symptoms" resulting from their service in Southeast Asia.[27] They continue to feel powerful emotions even though they initially suppressed these feelings. Depression, anger, anxiety, sleep disturbances, guilt feelings, flashbacks to Vietnam, psychic numbing, and emotional distance from loved ones are for many veterans the legacy of Vietnam.

Behavior patterns learned in Vietnam continued back in the world because there was no opportunity for any kind of debriefing. Survival tactics, effective in combat, were carried over into civilian life. Sometimes these behaviors lasted for years. Some vets, for example, would never leave home without a weapon. Most avoided crowds and were uncomfortable if anyone managed to get behind them. (Go to a restaurant with a Vietnam combat veteran and see who sits with his back to the wall.) For years after the war many continued to use ambush—avoidance techniques; they would never go to a place and return from it using the same route. Hyper alertness, the quality every infantryman needs to survive in combat, becomes exhausting when one is unable to relax—ever. One cannot approach the rest of life as if he were still walking point through hostile country. Some have been able to leave behind these behavior patterns; others have not.

The survival tactic that works best in combat is violence. When confronted with a hostile or emotionally threatening situation back in the world, quite a few vets resorted to what works. Barroom fights and violent behavior are not uncommon. Acts of violence have earned Vietnam veterans a disproportionately high representation among the prison population.

The prolonged stress of combat can be so severe as to "transform an individual into a survivor personality."[28] Indeed, the disruption may be so great that the stress can be "considered a personality disorder in its own right."[29]

In severe cases, the personality is almost "remade" by the experiences of combat. The impact of this kind of stress can be devastating, not only for the veteran, but for his loved ones as well.

A woman who snuggles close to her husband in bed as he sleeps does not expect a violent reaction to her tenderness; but many wives learned to their great sadness that you cannot touch a sleeping veteran without having him come immediately and aggressively back to consciousness.

《《——》》

BUSH-RELATED THERAPY

Though it has not been officially referred to in these terms, I believe the treatment model that has been most effective with the symptoms of delayed stress among veterans is "bush-related therapy." The experts (Lifton, Shatan, Wilson, Figley, and Meshad et al.) and the street therapists (vets and others who have become Vet Center counselors) are successful in dealing with delayed-stress symptoms only to the extent that they take seriously what happened in Vietnam "in the bush."

In the typical story of the Vietnam veteran approaching a VA psychiatrist, as already mentioned in Chapter 2, the veteran tells the doctor what is really bothering him. "Doc, I keep seeing the faces of these women and kids we killed." "I can't sleep at night ever since Vietnam." "I've been depressed since 'Nam." "I've held more than thirty jobs since I got out of the service. Something's wrong with me." "If my wife touches me while I'm asleep, I wake up choking her." The psychiatrist assumes the symptoms are really a manifestation of some disorder unrelated to combat and is unable, of course, to treat the patient. Bush-related therapy assumes that these symptoms are caused by Vietnam combat and have been reinforced by a bitter homecoming.

Once people begin to take a veteran's story seriously, he is emotionally free to confront the painful experience again, this time with a counselor or with others in a rap group. He is at last able to release emotions long buried. He can reinterpret events long past and integrate them with the rest of life. A rap group becomes a supportive, loving community and a surrogate for the friends he served with in Vietnam. In order to move beyond the war, to transcend its rage, guilt, and pain, the veteran must first remember, recount, confront, and reinterpret the painful incidents. This is an absolutely essential key to beginning the healing process.

The Vet Center treatment model is amazingly simple. Though widely resisted at first by mental health professionals, it has now won acceptance. More important, it works. Combat memories remain, of course, but they no longer dominate one's life. As one man put it, "The ghosts of the past are still there, but you learn to live with them."

Sometimes a vet's need is very simple: to grieve for a friend killed in action.

A former Army NCO walked into the San Diego Vet Center during the first month it was open. He had been with one of the earliest combat units in Vietnam in 1965-66 and had been a very close friend of his company's first sergeant. The "Top" was fatally wounded during an enemy attack, and he died in the vet's arms a few minutes later. The vet came into my office and said that he still felt the first sergeant's death very keenly, but he had never allowed himself to cry. He than began to sob. When he finished, he thanked me and left. He returned once more and did the same thing. When he left the second time, he said he would be fine. All he needed was to mourn his friend's death. I never saw him again.

Vets found the process of facing up to the impact of Vietnam difficult. The war itself had been so devastating that it seemed almost madness to think about it again, let alone discuss it in a rap group or with a counselor. But it soon became clear that "if the actual events didn't kill you, their ghosts won't, either." One man likened Vietnam to a chicken bone caught in the throat. The rap group provided him with the opportunity to cough up the bone and breathe again.

In the rap groups we remembered and interpreted the stories from Vietnam. Together we remembered how it was overseas. The rounds came in at Khe Sanh, fire bases were overrun, friends died in agony. Men wondered why it was that others died and they survived. A helicopter door gunner grieved that he hadn't been able to save some grunts on the ground. We relived atrocities, assassinations, and the murder of children. We suffered once again with each other the pain of coming back to the world. We listened to each other's stories of flashbacks, sleeplessness, and depression. We shared each other's anger and cynicism. The chicken bones came out, and people began to breathe again. The ghosts of Vietnam hovered—as they always would—but they were no longer lethal.

The Vet Center treatment model has proved effective. Hundreds of thousands of vets have been able to come to terms with the personal agony of Vietnam. The Vet Centers have been successful because they do not operate solely on the assumptions of traditional psychotherapy. Of course, counselors use sound and proved principles learned from psychology and the other social sciences, but they are not limited by these disciplines. They assist veterans to probe beyond the clinical issues and to reach the heart of the political, moral, and religious questions that lie at the heart of the Vietnam experience.

THE MORAL QUESTIONS

For years the mental health professions and the VA resisted the notion that Vietnam combat was a stress producer. Once the evidence became undeniable, delayed stress was accepted as a clinical disorder. The third edition of the *Diagnostic and Statistical Manual* (DSM III), the "psychiatrists' Bible," lists "posttraumatic stress" as an "anxiety disorder."[30] After the disorder was legitimized by inclusion within the diagnostic categories of DSM III, psychiatrists and other mental health professionals seemed less threatened by people who exhibited the symptoms. DSM III made it possible for combat-related stress to be taken seriously and treated. Researchers and clinicians wrote papers, lectured to professional groups, and reported the results of their work with veterans. Vietnam veterans were "in," and delayed stress had become fashionable. But therein lay a problem. Stress soon became the all-inclusive category that alone defined the relationship of the vets to the war they had fought. Stress completely encapsulated the vets.

Clark Smith was one of the first to understand this. He writes: "Stress is very much in vogue these days and it has swallowed the veteran whole." Smith recognized that continuing and profound stress in a variety of forms continues to plague Vietnam veterans. He believes that

> …psychologists discovered "post traumatic stress disorder," attributable in some undefined sense to all Vietnam veterans. This concept implied a fundamental notion: everyone could forget the war except the veteran who remained in a state of unresolved emotional conflict.[31]

Smith is convinced that the reduction of all symptoms to stress "promotes a psychiatric solution to the problems faced by Vietnam veterans." It also "de-politicizes the war."[32]

Smith correctly points out that much Vietnam stress is non-traumatic and that it is continuing rather than delayed. The enduring non-traumatic stress is the description that best fits Vietnam veterans. This stress resembles cynicism rather than psychological illness. The cynicism results from the recognition by veterans that they were according to Smith, *"in fact* betrayed by country and commanders."

Smith's analysis explores the role of psychotherapy in domesticating the war, "taming" it for the veteran and reducing its impact on the American public. Peter Marin is more explicit than Smith in his analysis of the true nature of the war's residue for the veterans. The title of his major contribution to the Vietnam literature betrays his point of view. For Marin the vets have continued "living in moral pain."[33]

Like Smith, Marin believes that the classification of a variety of emotional states found among veterans as mere symptoms of stress disorder clouds the real issue. "Feelings of guilt, perception of oneself as scapegoat, alienation from one's own feelings, an inability to love…especially when these appear individually and not as a set of interrelated symptoms" are, for Marin, symptoms of moral pain and not of clinical stress.[34]

Marin believes the categories of stress empty the vets' experience of its moral content and mask the true nature of the experience itself.

My own work with veterans has led me to the same conclusions reached by Marin and Smith. Some vets suffering from clinical symptoms of stress disorder (e.g., flashbacks, sleeplessness, depression) are unaware of any moral dilemma. Others, also afflicted with the same symptoms, suffer in addition a profound moral pain. On the other hand, vets with no clinical symptoms may also be afflicted with a deep moral and spiritual malaise.

Although these men are certainly not neurotic, they experience a pain that goes beyond survivor guilt (feelings of guilt because one survived combat while close friends did not). Moral guilt has nothing to do with survival. It is simply an awareness that one's own personal actions in the war were wrong. Moral guilt is also generated by the realization that the war itself was evil and one should not have participated in it. Guilt of this kind is by no means a clinical symptom. Quite the contrary, it results from a clearheaded analysis of one's past conduct with reference to some moral standard beyond one's own subjective feelings.

Anger and alienation, along with guilt, persist among vets as enduring qualities. Clark Smith's "soldier-cynic" is a familiar character for whom "it don't mean nothin'" has become a pervasive outlook on life. It would be a mistake to classify these deeply embedded attitudes as clinical symptoms of anxiety or stress disorder. Such attitudes are not pathological at all. They are appropriate reactions to the Vietnam War and the homecoming. This insight has been well expressed by veterans themselves in the classic one-liner "I'm not crazy; the war was fucked."

Clinical symptoms and moral distress are, of course, often interrelated. The faces that haunt a vet's dreams may be those of innocent women and children he killed. At the root of severe depression may lie memories of a village wantonly destroyed. Treatment of clinical symptoms does not necessarily alleviate the moral pain that arises from a new and deeper knowledge. What the vets now know, as Marin observes, is this:

> ...the world is real; the suffering of others is real; one's actions can sometimes irrevocably determine the destiny of others; the mistakes one makes are often transmuted directly into others' pain; there is sometimes no way to undo that pain—the dead remain dead, the maimed are forever maimed, and there is no way to deny one's responsibility or culpability, for those mistakes are written, forever and as if in fire, in others' flesh.[35]

The truth is that each veteran fought a different war in Vietnam and each must live with his own memories. For some there was only combat action against VC or NVA troops. For others there were atrocities, killing the innocent, and assassinations. For most, there is a strange and lingering ambivalence.

As often as not, this ambivalence relates to a profound and sometimes vague awareness that one has been immersed in evil. At the same time, remembering his combat experience, the vet realizes that he *liked* it. I've heard this said in many ways: "There's nothing like playing God!" "It's the only time in my life I was really alive!" "You live on the edge." "You decide whether people live or die."

In one of our first rap groups in the San Diego Vet Center, a veteran stood up and simulated holding an M-16. He swore to us that he truly loved the experience of "blowing away some motherfucking scum bag."

Often in counseling sessions or rap groups men recount events that cause both pain and exhilaration. These are examples of the "adrenaline rush" of combat that lingers for years in memory. There is nothing like the "combat high." Vets unwittingly yearn for it even though the same memories that bring the high also elicit painful images of death. Paradoxically, vets simultaneously cling to Vietnam and reject it. One can be, at the same time, emotionally addicted to combat, "stressed out" because of it, and morally repulsed by it. Psychotherapy can treat the addiction and the stress, but it leaves untouched the moral dimension.

Therapy deals with the emotional response to combat, but the moral questions require a deeper probing. One must go beyond both adrenaline rush and psychological stress to reach the moral realm. Exposure to evil on the scale of Vietnam irretrievably alters one's perceptions of the way life really is. More fundamentally, one's attitude toward oneself is irrevocably changed, as well. Alienation from others and even estrangement from the center of one's own soul are the aftermath of Vietnam combat. Healing this kind of moral pain demands a perception and language that therapy is unable to provide.

The soldier mentioned in Chapter 1 understood that prostitution was morally wrong and then quite logically asked how it was permissible by the same moral standard to "blow away gooks." He was caught in a dilemma that therapy alone cannot resolve. Though I never saw that young man again, I encountered hundreds like him in the years after the war. American moral standards (formed largely, though not exclusively, by our

Judaeo-Christian heritage) permit the taking of human life only in personal self-defense or in the defense of one's country against an aggressor nation. But the experience of most Americans who served in Vietnam was that the war had nothing to do with national self-defense. Many even felt that they were themselves the aggressors. As one vet told me, "I felt that we did to the Vietnamese what the Japanese did to the Filipinos in World War II." This is truly a moral dilemma that must be resolved beyond the bounds of psychotherapy.

Not surprisingly, veterans with no moral guilt—or very little—are those whose combat was against North Vietnamese troop units or VC guerillas. Personal self-defense is indeed the major issue in combat between opposing infantry. North Vietnamese soldiers became the aggressors who endangered the lives of Americans—as the Americans did to the North Vietnamese. Killing in that kind of combat carries with it very little, if any, guilt.

Quite different are the moral reflections of those aware of having been responsible for the deaths of innocent people. Caputo's realization that innocent blood was on his hands led him into deep moral anguish and a cry to God for forgiveness. Kovic's Marines, when they realized that they had fired into a hut and killed only old people and children, were overcome with shock and guilt. They began weeping and immediately crying out for the forgiveness of God. Greg Peters "stalked the perimeter" after the battle in which he killed dying enemy soldiers, "reciting the Act of Contrition and Hail Marys...begging God's forgiveness." The responses of grief and guilt described by Caputo, Kovic, and Peters are entirely appropriate to the situation.

The helicopter door gunner who described the "turkey shoot" to Mark Baker used different, more obscure, language to express guilt. He tells us that the fleeing Vietnamese civilians were "defenseless;" he remembers that "it was no better than lining people up on the edge of a ditch and shooting them in the back of the head." He recalls his own unforgettable adrenaline rush with the "insane thought, that I'm God and retribution is here, now, in the form of my machine gun…" His moral assessment is convoluted, though ultimately quite clear: "You begin to understand how genocide takes place. I considered myself a decent man, but I did mow those people down from my helicopter." He tried to compensate in his own mind that most of the people he was killing were the enemy, but he is really unconvinced by this. He then realized that you can "take anybody given the right circumstance and turn him into a wholesale killer." He finally admits that's what he was that morning. He considers it "bizarre."

The statement of Baker's door gunner is classic and almost paradigmatic for veterans who found themselves in similar situations and acted the same way. Men who "fired up villages," "blew away *mama-sans* and kids," or fragged their own leaders use similar language in their attempt to sort out what happened. At root, the dilemma that has become the dividing point of their lives is a moral one. Therapy may reduce some clinical symptoms, but it does not resolve the ache in the deepest regions of the soul.

BUSH-RELATED ETHICS

The journey out of the Vietnam night began in different ways for different veterans, but the journey remains incomplete without some resolution of the moral conflict. The war remains a moral issue not only for the vets but for all Americans. Healing for the veterans is inconceivable apart from a healing within society. The journey out of night, like the turning of America, must entail for all of us a real moral understanding of the war from the point of view of the soldiers who fought it.

Parades, the remaking of the American myth of war, and even psychotherapy do not resolve the issue; they only mask it. Caputo, Kovic, Peters, Baker's door gunner, and the thousands of vets they speak for must be heard. We must struggle through the moral issues with them, otherwise the war will truly have been in vain and history, too, must judge: "It don't mean nothin'."

The moral truth of war is hidden—deliberately, I suspect—in the writings of the pundits who see only global issues. Only an ethics that comes to terms with the realities of war from the viewpoint of its perpetrators and its victims is worthy of the name. In my dealings with other Vietnam veterans, I have come to understand the value of bush-related therapy as the only effective means of treating the psychological residue of combat. Even more important is a bush-related ethics that confronts the real moral struggles of the former soldier.

Bush-related ethics first takes one back in memory to the battlefield. The vet must remember as well as he can exactly what happened, allowing the feelings to come out but judging intellectually, as well. He must assess what he knew, understood, and felt at the time. The Vietnam literature we have examined often does exactly this. Vets do it in rap groups and counseling sessions. It is the necessary first step in arriving at a moral resolution.

Because war is ultimately an individual enterprise, each veteran must assume responsibility for what he did in combat. On the one hand, he must not allow himself to be enticed by well-intentioned therapists to consider that he was only a victim of the war. He must not "deresponsibilize" himself, evading the moral consequences of his actions. If he performed needless killings or committed atrocities, he must live with this truth about himself.

On the other hand, he must not accept personal responsibility for events beyond his control. The veteran must take into account the emotion of the moment, the combat rage—"going along with the program." He must distinguish this from gratuitous and cold-blooded killing. He must not "convict himself of first-degree murder if, in fact, it was second degree." Each former soldier must grapple with the moral questions of his own personal war. He must neither evade all responsibility nor assume too much. This kind of moral assessment is the essential prerequisite for coming to terms with Vietnam.

Assessment of individual responsibility in combat can never be divorced from the context of war; it is a moral sewer. Vietnam vets were largely teenagers drawn into a caldron of violence that had been planned, organized, and implemented by their own government with the endorsement of their elders. Military training had made of them efficient killers, and they had been turned loose in Vietnam to "do their thing." The war differed from previous American wars in that it was largely a guerrilla operation. The enemy that continually harassed and killed the GIs was, for the most part, indistinguishable from the civilian population, and so the troops lashed out murderously at Vietnamese civilians in retaliation. All Vietnamese became gooks, and the name of the game was to kill gooks wherever you found them. Some of the killing was, in fact, murder and atrocity. These individual acts are certainly the responsibility of the men who committed them, but the individual malice— hence guilt—is lessened considerably by several factors. The youth and moral immaturity of the soldiers caught up in mindless violence is one such factor, but another and more significant consideration is the constant stress they faced.

American soldiers in the field in Vietnam lived under conditions of chronic stress. They never knew when or by whom they would be attacked. Mortar attacks, booby traps, and land mines were ever-present possibilities, and the soldiers lived in a constant state of stress. Stress and fear reduce one's practical moral options. True freedom of choice lies at the heart of all morality; good or evil acts proceed ultimately and only from the exercise of free will. Factors such as stress and fear, which lessen freedom, also diminish responsibility.

Another significant determinant of moral responsibility is intellectual awareness at the time the act was committed. Prior training, level of moral development, and depth of insight are all factors that must be considered in assessing responsibility.

Philosophical and moral considerations of whether the war was right, whether we should have been in Vietnam, whether it was a just war, raised questions that did not seem to be the responsibility of soldiers to ponder. Presumably the society that cut their orders to Vietnam had already made the appropriate moral decisions, so the soldiers asked no questions—at first. Their commander in chief had told them to "bring the coonskin home." The average GI could hardly be expected to have sufficient intellectual and moral sophistication to resist the tide that carried him into combat and sometimes into murder and atrocity.

While the guilt of the Vietnam soldiers may be lessened considerably by the factors I have mentioned, no one knows better than they that a great deal of individual responsibility still rests on them for what happened overseas. No longer teenagers but now approaching middle age, many have discovered the need to go back and reexamine their role in the war. Until this is done, there can be no individual transformation, and the journey out of the night must remain unfinished.

Once a person has assumed the responsibility for past actions, then he or she is able to deal with guilt. In the guilt that grows out of war, there is always the recognition that one's actions have had irrevocable consequences. People are now dead who would still be alive if one had not pulled the trigger of an M-16 or fired the weapons of a Cobra gun ship or sprayed a village with napalm. Children are maimed and orphaned because of one's own personal actions. The consequences of these actions will last as long as the perpetrators and the survivors live. The guilt of war is the guilt of having been the bearer of death and terrible suffering to one's fellow humans.

This kind of guilt is not amenable to being neutralized by therapy. It, too, often turns to rage, depression, and self-destruction. The only solution is to make a conscious decision to turn one's life around. Guilt that simply lurks in the soul must be changed into an animating and driving force. The veteran's life must be changed, transformed. Whereas previously a man had been a bearer of death, he must now decide to become in his own way a bearer of life and peace. The drive, so powerful among veterans, to transform society, to "turn America around," is one of the ways this new transforming force shows itself. The desire for deeper, more sensitive personal relationships is another.

Classic moral and religious notions of guilt, repentance, and atonement are far more useful in dealing with such issues than is the narcissistic jargon of psychotherapy. Since leaving the Vet Center program, I have frequently been called on by the VA and by VA psychiatrists to conduct seminars and workshops for veterans and for those who work with vets. I have found that these classic moral and religious formulations have much meaning for vets who want to come to grips with the war's ultimate legacy—its moral and religious impact.

Quite a few vets who struggle with these major questions of ethics and religion are also afflicted with some posttraumatic stress symptoms. True healing for them entails a process that deals openly and unashamedly with the religious and moral character of their inner conflicts as well as with the stress symptoms. Despite the widespread indifference or hostility of psychiatry and psychology to matters of religion, there are some doctors who are both open to such issues and skilled in dealing with them. Contrary to stereotype, there are also clergy who are able to go beyond telling the vet that all his problems with

Vietnam will be over if he "accepts Jesus as his Lord and Savior." The Vet Center system and some of the VA hospital inpatient Viet-vet wards have begun some excellent programs that make use of sensitive and skilled doctors and clergy. In these settings vets are able to deal with the entire range of the war's residue.

A major difference between psychotherapy and traditional moral norms is the meaning of the word *conscience*. For Freud, conscience corresponded to the child's understanding of what his parents considered to be bad. This was established for each child by a system of rewards and punishments given in accordance with the attitudes of his parents or parental substitutes. Thus, getting dirty, expressing anger, enjoying sexual feelings, or any other set of attitudes and behaviors might be considered evil, depending on what the child has learned from his elders. For Freud, conscience performed the function of controlling and regulating impulses that, if left unchecked, would destroy society. These impulses are sex and aggression. Conscience in the Freudian conception is an unconscious conscience, functioning below the level of awareness. However much contemporary psychotherapy may part company with Freud, it has retained his basic notion of conscience.

Guilt in the context of psychotherapy is a feeling that results from experiencing whatever impulses, attitudes, or behaviors are forbidden within one's own personal system. There is no room for any real difference within this formulation between guilt feelings that arise from forbidden sexual

or aggressive impulses and guilt feelings that arise from the knowledge that one has committed wartime atrocities. Conversely, if one has "blown away" innocent women and children but experiences no unpleasant feelings about it, then there is no issue left to resolve.

Conscience, as it has been understood by moral philosophy in the Judeo-Christian religious tradition, is moral knowledge.

It is a judgment of the mind that some act or behavior is either good or evil. The mind measures a concrete situation against a set of values, then decides and acts. In the final phase of conscience, the mind either approves or disapproves of the decision. Guilt results from the awareness that one has disregarded the judgment of conscience and acted against a set of norms. Guilt is the enduring disapproval of conscience. It may or may not be accompanied by any feeling or emotion of guilt. In the Hebrew and Christian Scriptures, conscience is always related to God. Guilt is also connected to one's relationship with God.

If a person has performed evil actions, therapy requires that he or she undergo whatever treatment works for the alleviation of "symptoms" of guilt. The older tradition calls for atonement, the removal of the sin in the eyes of God, oneself, and the community, first through acknowledgment that one has sinned and then through some kind of restitution or act by which justice can be restored. The awareness that one has done evil—sin in the classical sense—requires repentance. The Greek word used in the New Testament for repentance means a "turning around of one's mind." This entails a complete turning away from the sin and a return to God. By repentance a person returns again to a love and concern for fellow humans and ultimately regains his own inner self.

WAR AND CONSCIENCE

War most often creates crises of conscience in both the traditional and therapeutic senses of the term. The prohibition against killing is both an internalized attitude learned from parental figures and a grave violation of the moral order.

Veterans have had experiences that produced spiritual deadening as well as psychic numbing. They carry around an altered perception of themselves. Many are alienated from their own spiritual center, from others, and ultimately from God. A person in this condition has lost his sense of self as a loving, moral human being. The only remedy is to regain a sense of self in loving relationships with others, to experience another transformation in self-perception. This is impossible solely within the confines of psychotherapy; it must be accomplished in the real world, the same world of suffering and death that produced Vietnam.

A decisive step in the journey out of the spiritual night of Vietnam is, as I have said, the acceptance of responsibility for one's own actions. But this is impossible without reference to some standard or norm against which actions can be measured. Finding common moral ground on any issue is very difficult in our culture, which fosters radical individualism and encourages each of us to operate autonomously within our own "space." Discovery of some useful, commonly understood ethical norms with respect to war is especially difficult. The long American love affair with violence and the notion that we must always "stand tall" in our relationships with other nations almost lead us to believe that war lies beyond moral judgment. Almost, but not quite. The war crimes trials at Nuremberg, the outrage over My Lai, and the Russian invasion of Afghanistan provide abundant evidence that we still think of war in terms of moral categories. Religious people throughout the world—Americans included—still contemplate war and evaluate its conduct with reference to their Scriptures and traditions.

The soldiers in the field asked questions about what they were doing in Vietnam precisely because they did hold some very deep moral and religious convictions. Many of those who lost their faith and became cynical did so because the guardians of the great moral and religious traditions failed to uphold those traditions. Atrocity, massacre, and ruthlessness are morally intolerable according to the very standards on which America is supposedly built. The soldiers understood this quite well, even if their spiritual guides, military leaders, teachers, and elders did not. A good number of combat soldiers also grasped intuitively the essential features of traditional moral standards concerning warfare. They carried with them into combat some notions of moral conduct in war. Many have suffered intense pain ever since the war because they believe they violated important ethical and religious norms. A glance at these standards is important.

JUST WAR

The Christian Church in the West and the secular society it helped to form have evolved a norm by which warfare is judged. Though the norm has been more often violated than observed during the fifteen centuries of its existence, it remains remarkably resilient as a standard against which acts of war may be reviewed and individuals held accountable. Its evolution owes much to St. Augustine, the bishop and theologian of North Africa who died in the fifth century. The early Christian Church was largely pacifistic. Christians at that time believed that engaging in armed combat was a violation of their conscience and represented a break from the teachings of Christ. But after the Christian faith emerged from the period of persecution and became the established religion of the Roman Empire, Christians began to view violence as sometimes necessary for the preservation of society. Especially when faced with the invasion of the "barbarian" tribes in Europe, new questions arose about whether and under what conditions warfare would be morally tolerable. Under the intellectual leadership of Augustine, the so-called just-war theory evolved.

Though borrowed in some measure from the secular society of the time, the just-war tradition was originally rooted in the Gospel. War was only tolerated as a last resort, and then only under very stringent conditions. The moral presumption was always against war, against the taking of human life. The under-pinning of the just-war theory was that war is only permissible if it is carried out in legitimate self-defense against an unjust aggressor. The first requisite of war was that its cause be just, that is, the protection of oneself, one's society, or innocent people. Other safeguards surrounded the permission to take up arms. The use of force must always be a last resort, taken only after all peaceful means of avoiding war have been exhausted. War must be declared by legitimate governmental authority and not be merely the result of individual or group whim. Before a society could take up arms, it had to have a reasonable hope of success in combat, otherwise war would amount to an irrational use of force. Consideration was given also to the intention of the combatants: the intent and the extent of the war must only be to fend off the aggressor and to preserve the society. Vengeance and the taking of the opponent's territory was never permissible.

Crucial to the just-war tradition was the notion of propor-tionality. This meant that there must be some proportion between the reason for which the war is fought on the one hand and the level of destruction and loss of life on the other. This first set of principles of the just-war tradition related to the war itself and the right of the state to go to war in the first place. The leaders of a country were held morally responsible for ensuring that these principles were safeguarded and followed. The indi-vidual citizen in a society was supposed to give his king and other leaders the benefit of the doubt, presuming that they were acting morally.

In democratic forms of government, which have emerged only during the past three or four centuries, sovereignty rests with the people of a nation. Given the wider dispersion of authority in democratic societies, the moral responsibility for ensuring that a war is just lies with the people as well as their leaders. Since the Protestant Reformation in the sixteenth century, the importance of the individual conscience in arriving at moral decisions has been emphasized in all Western societies. The arrival of democracy and the emphasis on individual conscience have redistributed the exclusive responsibility for approving and initiating warfare from the national leadership to the citizens of a society.

What we have seen of the just-war tradition so far relates to the war itself, determining whether it is justified and imposing responsibility on the leaders and the citizens—not the soldiers—for going to war in the first place.

A second set of principles governs the consciences of the soldiers who actually fight the battles. This second norm has nothing to do with the justice of the war or the rightness of the cause, but relates to the way the war is fought. Even soldiers fighting in an unjust war of aggression are bound by certain standards of conduct (the German soldiers who invaded Poland in 1939).

Two ideas undergird this second norm. The first is proportionality: the military means used in a battle or campaign—the destruction and killing—must be proportionate to the legitimate military objective. "It was necessary to destroy the village in order to save it," the notorious statement made by an army officer after he witnessed the destruction of a Vietnamese village, reflects a moral blindness and almost unbelievable insensitivity to this principle. The second moral consideration governing the conduct of soldiers in the field is the prohibition of attacks on noncombatants and nonmilitary targets. Traditional morality has always imposed on the soldier the serious obligation to avoid killing innocent civilians.

These were the moral standards the GIs carried with them to Vietnam—and that returned to haunt them in subsequent years. But the Vietnam generation grew up in the period immediately following the most blatant violations of just-war norms in the history of warfare. Nazi Germany initiated a war of aggression and employed tactics that were monumentally evil. The Allies rightly objected on moral grounds to Hitler's conduct of the war, especially the bombing of the civilian population of Britain. The Allies held the moral high ground in waging a defensive war against German and Japanese aggression.

Before long, however, the Allied powers themselves began to slaughter the civilian populations of Germany and Japan by bombing. The use of the atomic bomb against two Japanese cities resulted in the wholesale destruction of civilians and inaugurated the nuclear age. In the popular mind, the Allied violations of just-war morality were legitimized by the conviction that the war was a defense against the ruthless aggression of the Axis powers. The just cause of the war itself was believed to have excused the combatants from observing the moral conventions of warfare. Vietnam warriors were nurtured on the stories of World War II, and its moral lessons were not lost on them.

Judging World War II by the standards of the just-war tradition, there is no doubt that the Allies were justified in using military force to halt the German invasion of Poland, France, and the other European nations. The bombing of Pearl Harbor by the Japanese and their conquest of the Philippines were also acts of ruthless aggression, part of a strategy to achieve domination of the Pacific. The United States quite rightly used its massive military force in order to liberate the Philippines and halt Japanese expansion. The United States and its allies fought a "just war" according to the first set of traditional norms. But American and Allied conduct of the war, especially the bombing of civilian populations, was frequently immoral in terms of the second set of principles.

As an Army chaplain, priest, and VA employee, I have encountered quite a few World War II veterans who still struggle with guilt from battlefield incidents that happened long ago. Some feel remorse over killing enemy soldiers who were trying to surrender. Most of these men were acting under orders, because their unit was under fire and could not be burdened with prisoners; but some killed prisoners out of sheer desire for revenge. I know men who were artillery officers and members of bomber crews who feel some responsibility for the deaths of civilians. But however much these men may be troubled by their own actions or by what they saw others do, I have never met an American veteran of World War II who has any doubt that the cause in which he fought was just.

The case of Vietnam is quite different. Here the lingering moral doubts arise not just from the conduct of the war by soldiers in the field. The reason for which the war was fought, the cause itself, is questionable. Despite the rhetoric used by successive administrations about defending free peoples from the Communist menace, the fact is that the Vietcong consolidated their political base in the villages. The civilian population largely supported them and were in sympathy with their cause. Because of this widespread support of the VC and NVA in the villages, American soldiers were always at great risk from the civilian population. At this point, the moral legitimacy of the war became questionable. Who was really the aggressor if the people who live on the land supported the "enemy" cause?

Such a war cannot be won, and it should not be won because the only available strategy involves a war against civilians; and it should not be won, because the degree of civilian support that rules out alternative strategies also makes the guerrillas the legitimate rulers of the country. The struggle against them is an unjust struggle as well as one that can only be carried on unjustly. Fought by foreigners, it is a war of aggression; if by a local regime alone, it is an act of tyranny. The position of the anti-guerrilla forces has become doubly untenable.[36]

This, in fact, became the case in Vietnam. Rather than reexamine our policy, Presidents Johnson and Nixon resorted to deceiving the public. The light was always "at the end of the tunnel," or else there was some new policy that would work. In fact, the war was unwinnable because the South Vietnamese people supported the "enemy." At the point it became unwinnable, it also became immoral for two reasons: first, the war was no longer a defense against aggression, because the people who owned the land welcomed the so-called aggressors; second, the continuation of the war under those conditions led to the adoption of tactics that entailed widespread killing of noncombatants. The result was violence out of all proportion to any legitimate political end.

The continuing deception by American political leaders necessitated devising monstrously evil strategies for the conduct of the war in the field. The bombing and shelling of villages, the creation of "free fire zones" in which everything that moved was considered hostile, the use of defoliants, and the adopting of the "body count" as a criterion of success were all strategies devised by the military high command to satisfy their civilian superiors.

Thus, when the war became "unjust" according to the first set of principles, it became necessary to employ strategies and techniques that were immoral according to the second standard.

Enlisted soldiers and junior officers cannot be held responsible for the war itself or for the grand strategy employed to fight its campaigns and battles. We all know how democracy works. The government cannot wage war without the consent of the civilian population. Presidents Kennedy, Johnson, and Nixon conducted the war in Vietnam with the consent of the people and the Congress. Robert McNamara, Dean Rusk, and their successors at State and Defense crafted the policies that prolonged the conflict. General Westmoreland and the other senior commanders devised its major strategies and tactics.

While they do not bear the burden of determining whether the war should be fought or for devising its strategy, soldiers in the field are responsible for their piece of territory and for the people who come within range of their own weapons. They are not automatons or machines; nor are they mere technicians. They are never merely instruments of war or only its victims. "The trigger is always part of the gun, not part of the man."[37] Even under duress and when following orders there are opportunities for decision. The intoxication of combat does not completely overshadow the human capacity for acting freely.

The norms of a just war are important because they correspond to the common soldier's intuitions. Vets continue to struggle with their consciences precisely because they killed civilians, tortured and killed prisoners, destroyed villages, and committed other acts of unwarranted violence. Conscience reaches across the years with memories of deeds that transgressed sacred moral norms and violated deeply held convictions. It is almost as if the traditional conventions of warfare are engraved in the soldier's psyche.

The norms are a crucial backdrop against which to set one's own personal war story, for the veteran is not his own moral universe. The characters who haunt the veteran's dreams and perhaps even his waking hours—dead friends, buddies betrayed or saved, *mama-sans* and children, ARVN troops, the VC, and the NVA soldiers—were all real people, not just cameo figures crossing the stage of life. When their lives intersected the vets', the consequences were real and permanent. This violent collision of lives took place not within each vet's "inner space" but in the brutal and deadly world of hate and sin. The soldier's ethic, written somehow on the soul, liberates the veteran from a narcissistic retreat into the purely private domain of his own feelings.

Healing the psychic and spiritual wounds of war includes— but also requires more than—"getting in touch with your feelings" about it. The traditional war ethic is a reminder that one must remain in the real world, altering it in small ways, transforming it through one's own efforts, as far as possible edging it away from the monstrous evil of mindless violence.

The war ethic teaches something else, as well. Much of the resentment of vets against society arises from scapegoating and having the entire burden of the war thrust upon them. Once a person understands clearly the role and responsibility of the nation and its leaders in making war, he is freed from the inner necessity of shouldering the entire load. Rage, a reaction to this kind of scapegoating, is often found among vets as free floating and diffuse. A more nuance insight into the truth about shared responsibility for the war enables a vet to transform rage into constructively channeled anger. He is then able to say with a greater degree of confidence, "The war was fucked up, I'm not." More importantly, he is able to do something about it.

THE SIN OF THE WORLD

In theological terms, war is sin. This has nothing to do with whether a particular war is justified or whether isolated incidents in a soldier's war were right or wrong. The point is that war as a human enterprise is a matter of sin. It is a form of hatred for one's fellow human beings. It produces alienation from others and nihilism, and it ultimately represents a turning away from God.

Veterans and victims of war experience the sinful side of human nature as few others do. They come close to sin and are immersed in it. They acquire a "pervasive sense of suffering, injustice, and evil—a response to the world's condition that produces a feeling of despair, disgust."[38] Peter Marin calls this "the world's pain," and he believes that Vietnam veterans experience it as no others of our generation have.

Illusions are no longer possible when one's consciousness has been transformed by personal experience of evil on this scale. The brutality of the human condition is now a given of life, and one realizes that he is a part of it. Marin believes this "is far more than a therapeutic problem; it raises instead, for each of them, the fundamental questions of how to live, who to be."[39]

Night closes in on the spirit when all the comfortable assumptions about life are shattered by harsh experience. No bleakness of soul can compare with that born of the realization that evil lies close to the heart of all that is human. Evil is no longer the pale abstraction we make of it in our frantically upbeat, comfortable, and morally smug enclaves; it is, rather, the way we really are.

Spiritual darkness, as the vets have known it, is really an overpowering awareness of the extent of human sin. The biblical word for sin means "to miss the mark" or to fail to reach a goal or objective. In Scripture, sin is a personal act of free choice, but it is also the enduring condition of humanity. It is a turning away from God, from others, and from ourselves. Sin is, of course, a notion largely denied by our therapeutic culture.

War is the ultimate failure of humankind to reach the God-given objectives of maintaining love and justice in our relationships with each other and making a final turn to God. In our American past, the sinfulness of war has been masked by the cloak of righteousness and the glorification of violence for the sake of virtue. The Vietnam soldiers, unable to hide from the truth about war, were overpowered by the presence of sin.

In traditional Christian understanding, the recognition of sin is the necessary precondition for a new openness to God, for repentance—a turning around of one's inner self. The coming of God's kingdom and the "newness of life" promised in the New Testament are only possible after sin is named for what it is. Vietnam veterans have collectively experienced the connection between war and sin. Because of their public suffering, it is now possible for all Americans to see this connection. By their first steps in the journey out of spiritual darkness, the vets have pointed the way for all of us to embark on our own similar journeys.

ON THE WAY TO DEROS

The name of the game for a Vietnam vet is the same back in the world as it was overseas: make it to DEROS. The plane out of the 'Nam may have touched down at Travis or McChord years before, but full DEROS means achieving peace of mind and heart and soul back in the world. Sometimes this takes years, sometimes it happens overnight, and sometimes it never takes place. Full DEROS means coming out of the Vietnam night.

Like Randy Way, Langford Wells went through a long process. He was a platoon leader with an Army unit, and he returned from Vietnam an angry man. He looked at society with a great deal of rage at "the trivial, inane, bullshit things" that went on. He found that he was still a combat junkie, so he became a cop. As he met other vets and began to talk with them about Vietnam, he found that this stage passed, and the rage diminished.

Then he began to remember an incident that occurred in Vietnam. When he was wounded, the medic who attended him looked into his eyes and seemed to see all the way to his soul. The medic simply said, "It's a minor wound," and went on his way. Wells remembered the incident years later back in the world, and somehow that fleeting moment exerted a power over him. He began to reach into the more sensitive side of his own nature, which had been numbed by the war.

At this point, Wells was able to look at the moral and religious questions that had troubled him. He worked his way out of the "warrior cult" that had trapped him for so long. His resolve to contribute "to the fabric of society" has become a point of moral obligation. He does this through his law enforcement job, which he now sees in a different way. He is no longer a combat junkie but a man attempting to better society. He has not returned to the religious practice of his Catholic faith, but he can once again see a presence of God in his life and in the world.

When the moment was right for him, Wells decisively, symbolically, and very effectively made his DEROS from Vietnam complete. He "cut a set of orders" for himself on his own typewriter. These orders contained all the correct military jargon with name, rank, service number, unit. He simply relieved himself from duty in Vietnam. He feels relieved from the responsibility of staying awake nights, waiting for the next combat action; he no longer must worry about his men—many of whom are dead—or bear the other burdens of the war. Wells has posted his orders on the wall of his bedroom and looks at them often. He's now back in the world.

Jack Lyon, the first president of the Vietnam Veterans of San Diego, was a Marine Corps captain. Like any good officer, he assumed responsibility for his men in Vietnam. In the action for which he was awarded the Silver Star, he lost some of his men. He himself was wounded. After his return from overseas, he suffered from many of the stress-related symptoms common to vets. He also became addicted to drugs. He went through a drug treatment program, got clean, and stayed clean. He then worked through the stress problems at the Vet Center and immediately emerged as a leader among the vets. "Captain Jack" became not only a political leader but a man whom vets in trouble often called upon. He became as skilled in doing "therapy" as any counselor I've seen. He accomplished all this while operating his own business.

Lyon sees his own moral obligation as one of making a real imprint on the political and social system. Having made significant local contributions himself, he is now more concerned with national issues, primarily those connected with justice and peace. He believes Vietnam vets must wake the country up to the realities of war. He worries that another generation of "kids" is being seduced by an administration that seems determined to lead the country into war. Jack Lyon, too, sees the psychological, moral, and spiritual dimensions of life as inseparable. He has become deeply committed to his own personal spiritual program.

Steve Mason, a veteran of Vietnam combat with the Special Forces—the Green Berets—is the national poet laureate of the Vietnam Veterans of America. The moral thrust of his life has become an attempt to "turn America" away from war. Mason believes that the vets have something to say to the nation about war, a unique perspective. Until the vets speak out and the nation listens, there is no closure on the war. He writes:

> ...America is waiting for us, now. And the world is waiting for America. It won't be enough to wear buttons. It won't be enough to coach a girl's softball team when the children of other poor men are too weak to stand. It's our play now. The truth of our perspective must be assimilated by our nation's system of values. And added to the consciousness of the world.
>
> Until then, no closure.[40]

For Mason

> there remains one, much needed war.
> One, last commitment worthy of a lifetime—to fight
> for peace in each of our hearts against the fierce enemies
> of our darkest natures.
> And to march in lock-step with veterans of all wars from
> all nations for human dignity.
> Then shall we pass in review and each will hear
> mankind whisper to the gods,
> "There then, goes one of ours."[41]

REDEMPTION AND HOPE

Healing for each individual entails something unique. A vet must deal with his own past. This is what he brings to enrich the community. But each vet, by working through his own moral pain, brings to the larger society the gift of moral seriousness. The "turning of America" requires a retreat from the triviality that threatens to consume us. The Vietnam veterans' story, troublesome though it may be to America, is nonetheless salutary because it calls us once again to consider the importance of life and to remember that our actions have consequences beyond ourselves.

Even in its Achilles heel, the journey of the vets is instructive. The great flaw, the area that remains largely unexplored by the vets, is their relationship with the Vietnamese people, both here and in Vietnam. Unfortunately, the "gook syndrome" remains embedded in many veterans' hearts. But this may be changing, too. A few vets have already returned to Vietnam through the efforts of the VVA. Many more have begun to purge their own souls of the residue of hatred. In this regard, Peter Marin writes:

> For decades now, we have considered Buber's 'I-thou' relationship the ideal model: a respectful intimacy in which the integrity of the other is not violated as the other's nature is fully perceived, understood, and embraced. No doubt all of that is necessary and good. But it is also morally insufficient. It is incomplete. For it does not fully take into account the inevitable presence of the invisible others, the distant witnesses: those who have suffered our past acts and those who may suffer them in the future.
>
> The proper consideration... is "I-thou-they:" the recognition that whatever we do or do not do in our

encounters, whatever we forget or remember, whatever truths we keep alive or lies we fabricate will help form a world inhabited by others. Our actions will play a significant part in defining not only the social and moral life of our own people, but the future of countless and distant others as well, whose names we will not know and whose faces we will not see until perhaps, a decade from now, other American children view them through the sights of guns.[42]

The more sensitive vets have already made the connection between the Vietnam War and future wars. A significant number of men and women are actively involved in the effort to prevent the administration from beginning another Vietnam in Central America.

Of course, the possibility is always there that a large number of veterans will succumb once again to the mythology of war. Current attitudes in America are very powerful. It is, after all, good to be "standing tall" again. Many who saw duty in Vietnam seem to be persuaded once more by the rhetoric. "We really could have done it if they'd only let us."

It is also possible that a majority of Vietnam vets will follow the lead of a great many World War II vets by "sealing over" the moral issues of war sitting around a VFW hall drinking beer and swapping stories about the glory days. The future is always open-ended.

In my experience, those who have come closest to achieving the kind of personal and communal healing we have been considering are those who have transformed their lives through a spiritual journey of some kind. Having been touched by the pain and sin of the world, these people have attempted to respond as healers themselves.

Healing in the complete sense for these men and for countless others like them consists in more than dealing with the psychic residue of war. Bush-related therapy was a necessary but insufficient element in their healing process. Beyond therapy, each one of them has come to grips with the moral questions of their war. Each has in some way reached out to become himself a healer of others. Redemption of their own lives has been intimately connected with being a bearer of healing and hope to other vets and to the country they love.

THE VETS AS PROPHETS

Biblical prophecy did not emphasize the foretelling of future events. Rather, the prophets were those who spoke the word of God to the people of Israel, reproving them for their infidelities against God's covenant and reminding them that God had called them to a moral life. War, injustice, and oppression were grist for the prophets' utterances. Vietnam vets, though obviously not aware of any divinely given mission to society, speak a word of prophecy in their collective story, and especially in their spiritual journey, to a nation that purports to base its existence on biblical teachings. The nation that believes itself to be morally correct in all that it does would do well to learn from the bitter anguish of those who fell from grace while doing its bidding.

The Vietnam soldiers forced America to face the fact that war is primarily a moral issue. It is really a series of individual moral acts, some good and some evil, but all partaking of the sinfulness of war itself. The myth of glorious war rings hollow after Vietnam. War in the cause of virtue makes as much sense now as does sex for the sake of virginity. Sergeant Stryker and Rambo still flicker across our screens, but after Vietnam, they are as real as Alice in Wonderland.

The plight of the combat vets unmasks a particular hypocrisy that surrounds war in our time. We accept the delusion that high-tech tools allow us to fight a clean war. B-52 strikes, the spraying of napalm, artillery strikes punched in miles away from point of impact, sanitize the killing. As Caputo observed, in Vietnam "ethics seemed to be a matter of distance and technology."

The true nature of war is further hidden in our culture by the bureaucratic process necessary to plan it and the management techniques employed to supervise it. Those actually responsible for the conduct of a war are now involved only in a process of planning, analysis, and management. They take no risks, confront no death, and allow themselves to evade the moral burden of what they do. People, the enemy, the civilian populations, and our own soldiers are simply numbers and instruments in their calculations.[43]

This was demonstrated most poignantly at a meeting in St. Louis in 1979 of those who would be responsible for establishing the Vet Centers. Most of us at the session were Vietnam vets, but we had several guest speakers, most prominent among them being Leslie Gelb, who had been a Pentagon analyst and *New York Times* reporter. We had just finished watching some footage actually filmed in Vietnam in which an infantry point man is killed right on camera. When the film ended, the emotion was at a peak. No one could speak. Tears were in everyone's eyes. It was then Dr. Gelb's turn to speak. Someone in the audience asked him whether he thought the soldiers who actually fought the war were really just pawns in the minds of those who did the planning. Gelb's reply was a brutally honest and unforgettable single word: "Yes." The room came "unglued." People began sobbing openly when they heard the truth they had always suspected.

I believe that high-tech killing and the amoral processes employed by politicians, planners, and the senior military constitute a web of delusion that continues to mask the nature of war. In Vietnam, the combat soldier alone saw death up close; his story alone tells the moral truth.

The impact of Vietnam for the veterans who actually fought—psychic stress, moral confusion, and the dark night of the spirit are the true costs of war. The voice of the veteran is raised in protest against the prevailing currents of our culture; it unmasks our delusions. It is a voice of prophecy we fail to heed at our peril. The vets remind us that we also sit in the shadow of darkness, imprisoned by our own moral confusion and stress, each in our own private space immersed in our personal concern with little relationship to community. We who have been able to trivialize even war can do little else with moral seriousness. The voice of the vets is a call to discover a deeper ethic, a richer way of life; it is a voice of healing.

CHAPTER FIVE:
THE A.W.O.L. GOD

The central religious question to come out of the war is the one raised at the beginning of this book: "Where was God in Vietnam?" When vets ask it, the question carries an element of rage directed against God. Like most Americans, vets have a religious impulse buried deep within their souls. Like most of us, they believed in God; they also believed that God is good and just. But where was God at Khe Sanh? What was He doing during the Tet offensive? Why didn't He come along on search-and-destroy missions? Where was He at My Lai and when other atrocities were committed? If God can do no better in governing the world than to allow what happened in Vietnam, then either He is not really there at all—nowhere to be found in the vacant universe—or else He is truly evil and capricious. He is no longer deserving of faith, and so faith becomes impossible.

The loss of religious faith, so widespread among vets, bears no likeness to the sterile and bloodless agnosticism of the university campus. Nor does it resemble the simple non-consideration of the "God question" that pervades so much of American life. On the contrary, the veterans' rejection of God is active, passionate, almost physical, and rooted in the best of reasons. They have been betrayed. On some level, they had believed that

God had promised something and then didn't or couldn't deliver. He would be with them, they thought, as they went through Southeast Asia; yet He wasn't. He was hiding, malignantly absent from a situation that demanded a loving, caring, or at the very least, a just God. But God went AWOL in Vietnam, and for many vets whose lives have been ripped apart at the core and who have lost the power to believe and hope, he has not yet reported back.

Vietnam was the experience of the madness of war. Human goodness was subverted on every side. Men sank into a sewer of depravity. Caputo writes that "it was the dawn of creation in the Indochina bush, an ethical as well as a geographical wilderness."[44] Caputo tells the truth: "Out there, lacking restraints, sanctioned to kill, confronted by a hostile country and a relentless enemy, we sank into a brutish state."[45]

A moral discovery so many soldiers made in Vietnam was of their own limitless capacity for malice, and by extrapolation, the unsuspected depths and pervasive nature of human depravity. The religious discovery followed hard upon the first. Where is redemption, grace, and the goodness of God in such a caldron of madness, savagery, and malice?

When one is forced to confront the issue of God and evil with both head and heart, the impact is always severe. The experience of evil is *so* profound, that one *must* look at a "good" God, our Heavenly Father, and come to the conclusion that either He is *not* good, or that two contradictions *can* exist side by side. In either case, one's religious faith can never be the same again. It is either deepened or completely destroyed. Indeed, veterans of Vietnam seem to have come out of the experience with religious faith on a different level or with no faith at all. "It don't mean nothin'" on the lips of a great many vets applies preeminently to God and to anything connected with religion.

GOD IN THE BUSH

Bush-related therapy and ethics take seriously the psychological and moral issues that arise in combat. So, too, does a bush-related theology. The starting point for any serious exploration of God's absence from the world in the face of evil must be found within the experience of evil itself. The war stories told in this book provide just such an experiential context. The vets' stories reveal clearly a nihilism so deep that it cannot but extend to religious faith.

Yet the story is many-sided. It is not only about a loss of faith but also about the desperate struggle to find God in the midst of hell. In spite of lengthening shadows of despair and doubt, soldiers in the field often sought God, wanting nothing more than to experience touches of His mercy, forgiveness, and above all, deliverance from evil.

I found in my own travels in Vietnam that soldiers were glad to see the chaplain for a variety of reasons. Mass or any religious service on a fire base or in a jungle clearing with an infantry company brought all kinds of men to worship, some of whom hadn't been to church in quite a while. In the rear areas of Vietnam, as well, men turned out for prayer and worship with a sense of eternity's proximity, the nearness of death. As the twelfth-century mystic Bernard of Clairveaux remarked, we live "at the edge of eternity." Nowhere more than in a combat zone does one sense the truth of this statement. Men become aware of their own mortality. For both the chaplain and the men, each religious service might be his last. One indeed focuses on God more keenly in this setting.

At the same time, the old adage "There are no atheists in a foxhole" is not true. There are plenty of them. Some were nonbelievers before coming to Vietnam, but most often they were men who had lost their faith because of what they experienced—proof that a foxhole can make an atheist out of a believer.

Some men found God in new and more profound ways because of their Vietnam experience. David Rioux was such a man. One of two brothers who served at the same time and for a while in the same company in combat, David was terribly wounded. Maimed in one leg and one arm, the most severe result of his wounds was total blindness. A devout Catholic before the war, David never lost his faith in America, its reason for fighting in Vietnam, or most importantly, his religious faith. It seems that his "interwoven faith in God, country and the justness of the cause" sustained him in the midst of his suffering. Though severely injured and blinded, David Rioux went on to earn a doctorate in philosophy. His brother, Michel, with whom he shared so much Vietnam combat, said of him, "What he suffers, he suffers for good reasons. If he didn't believe in anything—if he were an agnostic or an atheist—he'd have pretty good reason to commit suicide. It's this faith that gives him the strength he needs."[46]

David Rioux told the authors of *Charlie Company,* the book that published his story:

> "Michel and I saw clearly a lot of things that other people didn't see. We both knew why we were in Vietnam, and the men around us didn't, for the most part, or saw it only confusedly, but we saw why we were there and we were proud to be there, defending a people who were being oppressed by Marxist Communism. We were doing something that was commendable in the eyes of God, our country and our family…"[47]

The authors conclude that David was "as prepared to live in darkness as he had been to die for that belief." A large statue of Mary, Queen of Heaven, adorns his study, and the authors note that "David Rioux in his blindness had plainly found shelter in her sight."[48]

Such profound religious faith is not common among Americans. David Rioux's story is singular in the extraordinary sustaining power of his faith, which apparently preserved him even from the depression and anger that ordinarily accompany blindness. But David is not unusual among veterans in that his faith in God was interwoven with belief in country and in the justice of its cause. And for many vets the weave between God and country unravels first.

Another man who served in Charlie Company, one of its commanding officers, Richard Lee Rogers, also made the connection between God and country. He felt that Vietnam had "made him a stronger man by deepening his commitment to Christ and helping him, through prayer, to master the fears he sensed in himself and saw in other men. 'I asked God not to let me be a coward,' Rogers said, 'and He did not.'"[49]

Not every vet who preserved his religious faith remained a staunch supporter of the American fight against communism in Vietnam. Greg Peters still hears "Thou shalt not kill" ringing in his ears. He believes the commandment means what it says and that the prohibition against killing extends even to Communists, but he has come to realize that God is merciful, forgiving all our sins, including those committed in war. He also feels that he has a better understanding of the cross of Christ after Vietnam. He grasps, now in a way that he never could before Vietnam, Christ's command to "Love one another as I have loved you." The border around his license plate reads: "Hug a Russian." When he told me that, I laughed. His reply was "It's better than killing them."

I have talked with a number of vets like these men whose religious faith survived Vietnam. For some, there was a period of estrangement from religion followed by a period of searching and, finally, a return to the worship of God, if not to a church.

For others, faith was never laid aside but reached deeper levels because of Vietnam. Still others returned from their tour more or less in the same place religiously as they were before going overseas.

Most Vietnam vets with whom I have discussed religion, however, have simply lost their faith. Many still believe in some kind of God but are either angry at Him or don't see how He could be a personal God. Others are now agnostic or atheistic. This is not merely the cultural erosion of faith common in our society. It is a direct result of Vietnam.

The vets' own stories are remarkable on this point. I am impressed by the consistency in their statements. "I used to be an altar boy." "I went to Sunday school regularly." "I was religious." "I went to church." "I believed in God." The punch lines of the stories run something like this: "But I haven't been to church since Vietnam." "I don't believe in God since 'Nam." "I haven't been near a church since I was wounded."

Mike MacDonald's Catholic faith died on the battlefield in Vietnam. His story is typical.

> His (Mike's) belief in God was as surely a casualty of the war as his trust in the word of his government. The boy who had gone to mass every morning in Minneapolis could not sustain his faith surrounded by the random and, for him, meaningless carnage of Vietnam; not even his own survival was evidence for him that God lived and cared.
>
> "It's nice to say someone is looking out after me," he said, "but the reason I made it was nothing more than blind fucking luck. Why does the mortar hit the guy next to you and not you, if you're in the killing radius? I don't think there's anything that God did, if there *was* a God.
>
> It was just luck." His mother's insistently pious let-

ters began accordingly to be a trial for him to respond to. Once, he took some to a chaplain and asked, "How do I answer this?"

"You're not the only one," the padre answered, reading his doubts. "All of our faith gets tested out here."

Mine is no longer being tested, MacDonald thought. *It's gone.*[50]

Like MacDonald, another ex-infantryman and ex-Christian reports:

> We became the animal in the jungle. We got in touch with the other side of our human potential and it terrified us. The Nam put an incredible blockage in me in relation to God—I just didn't feel that God loved me. I had a complete loss of faith in the Nam.[51]

Years of experience in veteran rap groups and thousands of counseling sessions with vets led me to conclude that loss of religious faith in Vietnam was the norm rather than the exception.

Ironically, loss of faith was often accelerated by contact with the men whose task was to proclaim God's presence on the battlefield: the chaplains.

GOD AND THE CHAPLAINS

The story of the military chaplaincy as it performed in Vietnam has never been told. I mention the role of the chaplaincy because it bears directly on the way soldiers related to their faith. Not that chaplains were central to military operations; we were not. But the chaplains represent religion in a way that no one else can. Soldiers can always read what the military uniform says about a person; the chaplain's uniform is illustrative. On the left collar of his combat fatigue uniform the chaplain wears the Christian cross or the Jewish tablets of the law. The uniform accurately reflects his function. He is a pastor to those who share his religious faith and counselor to all the troops. He performs the same duties as his civilian counterparts in congregations back home. But he also does far more. He must be present with his troops before, during, and after the battle. He must pray with them and for them. Most important, he must prepare them for death through last rites and prayer, which in Vietnam could be at any time or any place and would certainly be brutal. This is the historical role of the military chaplaincy. In Vietnam, as in previous wars, chaplains performed those functions quite well.

The real problem with the military chaplaincy in Vietnam had little to do with these traditional functions. Rather, the issue lay elsewhere. Symbols speak loudly: while the chaplain wears his religious insignia on the left collar of his battle dress, he displays on his right shoulder the insignia of military rank. He is an officer in the Army, Navy, or Air Force. He is, like the soldiers themselves and their military commanders, an integral part of the "green machine," the Army. He is seen as inseparable from the basic function of the green machine, which is killing.

In our previous wars, no one questioned the relationship between the religious and military roles of chaplains. The reason, of course, is that in previous wars there was little doubt in anyone's mind that the fight was a noble sacrifice of almost religious dimensions. *Pro Deo et Patria* (For God and Country), the motto of the Army Chaplain Corps, was accepted as entirely appropriate because there was no perceived disjunction between the intention of God and the American cause.

What happened in Vietnam amounted to nothing less than a complete collapse of the link between God and country. The chaplain represented a system of mixed and no longer meaningful symbols. A man who believed "the war sucks" and who also wanted to know "Where is God?" put the chaplain in the same category with other lifers. Most likely, he viewed the chaplain as a "sheep in wolf's clothing"[52] and resented him even more than the others. I have experienced a good bit of resentment from vets simply because I served as a chaplain in Vietnam.

The tragic failure of the military chaplaincy in Vietnam was its lack of perception of the real issues involved in the war. Because chaplains were, for the most part, operating out of the same religious assumptions as the troops, our discernment of what was truly at stake came too late.

The bitterness of the men toward chaplains resulted from our failure to discern the moral and religious meaning of what was taking place. The men, both as soldiers during their combat tour and as veterans after the war, have been looking for moral guidance and spiritual direction, but they have received neither. The clergy, whose classic and traditional role has been to provide just such guidance, failed to do so, and the vets still resent it.

Part of the problem lay in the training of chaplains both during the basic officer course and in chaplain seminars and course offerings subsequent to the initial training. During the 1960s and early 1970s, the military chaplaincy, like much of the civilian clergy, indulged in a virtual orgy of psychological training. Group dynamics, training as facilitators, Sensitivity and awareness seminars, all helped us to be more caring and relevant but of course evaded real moral and religious issues. Although chaplains are not expected to be theological scholars or moral philosophers, they should know these subjects in some depth if they are to provide guidance for the troops. I remember only one chaplain conference that was devoted to theological rather than psychological themes during my three-year tour in the army. It was the last conference I attended before discharge. The Vietnam War was almost over. The chaplaincy began to learn too late for the Vietnam soldiers.

Let us return to the soldier who juxtaposed the supposed moral legitimacy of killing Vietnamese with the prohibition of prostitution. He asked a profound moral question. The answer I gave him was partially correct. In terms of Christian just-war teaching, he could kill Vietcong and NVA soldiers—who at that time were causing our unit some real problems—because the alternative to his killing others would likely be his own death or the deaths of his buddies. Both the question and the answer come out of a "between the rock and a hard place" moral situation.

Beyond both the question and the answer, however, lies a troublesome religious awareness. Even though killing enemy soldiers amounts to legitimate self-defense in a combat zone, something about it is very wrong. The harsh reality of combat may leave the individual no choice but to kill in a given situation, but the GI survivor knows somehow that both he and his dead enemy have been sucked into unspeakable evil, that is, sin. The New Testament is unequivocal on this point. Soldiers from a Christian background and Christian chaplains all knew this at least by way of religious intuition.

Despite the neat arguments of the just-war doctrine, there is a larger context in which war can never be justified. War, more than any other human undertaking, validates and verifies the notion of "original sin," or the "sin of the world." This religious intuition lurks behind all our notions about self-defense, the legitimacy of taking another's life to preserve our own, and the necessity of defending against unjust aggression. Killing in combat may be morally permissible, but the permission is always ambiguous and always arises from a situation that can only be characterized as "total immersion" in evil.

I believe the essential failure of the chaplaincy in Vietnam was its inability to name the reality for what it was. We should first have called it sin, admitted we were in a morally ambiguous and religiously tenuous situation, and then gone on to deal with the harsh reality of the soldier's life. I do not believe that a Christian chaplain can legitimately go beyond the toleration of killing in immediate self-defense. He errs if he tries in any way beyond that to supply religious motivation for the soldiers to "carry on the struggle."

The "chaplain bullshit" the troops resented was, in fact, this kind of religious hype: "Oh, God, let us struggle mightily against thine enemies." This amounted to endorsement of the war in the name of religion. Memorial services for dead comrades with empty boots and M-16s stuck in the ground were apparently occasions for much of this kind of "chaplain bullshit" either because the chaplain said the words himself or the commander did, while the chaplain stood silently by. Truthfully, though, it is as difficult for the chaplain as for anyone else in the unit not to wish vengeance and the punishment of God upon the enemy who have killed "his" troops.

The only way I could ever find to resolve—at least in part— the chaplain's dilemma was to admit with the troops that the "whole goddamn war is fucked." Translated theologically, this comes out as we are surrounded by "the sin of the world" and we, too, are sinful creatures.

Everyone knew and sang a song in Vietnam in those days that began with the line "We've got to get out of this place." I always thought that fit nicely with the petition in the Lord's prayer "Deliver us from evil." An emphasis of that kind in talking with the men, both individually and in sermons, seemed to avoid some of the distortions of Christian faith that were inevitable in Vietnam.

There is another side to the chaplaincy as it functioned in Vietnam. The chaplain brought significant spiritual gifts to the troops: celebration of a Protestant worship service or offering mass in a jungle clearing or on a fire base. We prayed the Lord's Prayer with the men. We joined with them in a serious cry to God to deliver us all from a terrible evil. We brought some sense of God's forgiving presence, even in the midst of madness and savagery. Chaplains had much to do with preserving and deepening the faith of many and prepared thousands for their entry into eternity. Chaplains tried to bring the consoling presence of God into the most horrible situation any of us had ever faced. This is, on balance, no small thing. Finally, whatever we may have done wrong, we did risk our lives to be with the troops; some chaplains died and many more were wounded in the attempt to be pastors to the men and women in Vietnam. This has to count for something.

Criticism of the chaplaincy arises largely because we did not grasp and articulate the moral and religious implications of Vietnam. We failed to provide the kind of spiritual direction the men really needed. Tragically, We earned the enduring resentment of many of the troops we loved and served. We unwittingly contributed in some measure to their loss of faith precisely because *we were blind* to *the sin of war,* and therefore implicitly condoned it.

The relationship of the chaplaincy and lost faith is a recurring theme. Jeffrey Dube interviewed a psychologist at a VA Medical Center in New England, a man with experience and skill in dealing with "posttraumatic stress disorder." The psychologist told Dube about the veterans' dealings with chaplains: Most of the comments were quite negative.

> The view was that these chaplains were just regular 'lifers' with a typical attitude toward the grunt. The chaplains just wanted to minimize or discount the problem of healing the horrors that went on in combat, and the soldier's feelings about what went on in the war. The chaplains' attitude was basically a "carry on the

good work, soldier" or "numb" the pain, or try to "stuff it" away. Over the years I have dealt with many of these vets who came from very religious homes and backgrounds. They ended up in "the Nam" as infantry and felt *totally* let down not only by the experiences of how they viewed themselves in relation to God, but also their notions of God. These guys were really struggling with what they had believed in their homes and environments. This remains a struggle for them today. So now, what do they believe?[53]

The same psychologist believes that the vets' contact with a chaplain could have "either a positive or negative effect" on the soldier. "How did the chaplain respond to the soldier? Did he acknowledge the pain? The confusion? The questioning? Or did he just try to smooth it over? The questioning has not stopped..."[54]

Michel Herr captures the irony of the chaplains' prayers and the role of religion in the war.

Prayers in the Delta, prayers in the Highlands, prayers in the Marine Bunkers of the "frontier" facing the DMZ, and for every prayer there was a counter-prayer—it was hard to see who had the edge...

In wood paneled, air-conditioned chapels in Saigon, MACV padres would fire one up to sweet muscular Jesus, blessing ammo dumps and 105s and officer's clubs. The best-armed patrols in history went out after services to feed smoke to people whose priest could let themselves burn down to consecrated ash on street corners...

Sermonettes came over Armed Forces radio every couple of hours, once I heard a chaplain from the 9th Division starting up, "Oh, Gawd, help us to learn to live with Thee in a more dynamic way in these perilous time, that we may better serve Thee in the struggle against Thine enemies....[55]

Robert Jay Lifton always a careful and astute listener, reaches the heart of the problem and employs a neat turn of phrase to express it:

> The men had a special kind of anger best described as ironic rage toward two types of professionals...chaplains and "shrinks." They talked about chaplains with great anger and resentment as having blessed the troops, their mission, their guns and their killing: "Whatever we were doing—murder, atrocities—God was always on our side."
>
> In that sense chaplains and psychiatrists formed an unholy alliance not only with the military command but also with the more corruptible elements in the soldier's psyche.
>
> We can then speak of the existence of a "counterfeit universe" in which pervasive, spiritually reinforced inner corruption becomes the price of survival...[56]

It is to the "counterfeit universe," a place of "spiritually reinforced inner corruption," that we now turn.

JESUS CHRIST AND JOHN WAYNE

When I first became aware of the extent to which the loss of faith among vets had grown, I had no mental peg on which to hang what I was learning. I knew only that Vietnam had been harmful to the souls of the ex-GIs with whom I had been dealing. One Tuesday evening during our weekly combat-vet rap group at the San Diego Vet Center, some pieces of the picture fell into place.

The rap group had just been through some heavy stuff. Talk had turned, as it usually did, to what it all meant. Why were we there? Why did I make it back and so many others didn't? What or whom could you believe after Vietnam? Most of the dozen or so veterans present agreed that Vietnam had caused them to lose their faith in "the system." This meant they didn't believe the government, politicians, business leaders, or God. One ex-Army officer had observed that they had lost their faith precisely because they had bought into the system so heavily before going overseas. The war had unmasked the system, revealing it in all its nakedness.

At this point in the discussion the door gunner spoke up. He was an unforgettable man, given to colorful and descriptive speech. He had served his time with an army combat unit as a helicopter door gunner. "Before I went to Vietnam," he said, "I believed in Jesus Christ and John Wayne, but in Vietnam both went down the tubes." He had said it for them all.

The door gunner's choice of imagery, "Jesus Christ and John Wayne," was perfect. He was a former Catholic, an altar boy. He knew quite a bit about Jesus Christ, but he believed that Jesus Christ operated in a certain way: always within the context of American life—he made "the system" work. He endorsed life the way it was, and he held the promise of eternal happiness if you hung in there. Jesus Christ was the man who could make it turn out all right.

If you wanted to see how God wanted everything to work out here below, watch John Wayne, the archetypal American—rugged, powerful, a fighter, but virtuous, good, and religious in his own way. John Wayne never started trouble, but when it came, he met it vigorously and aggressively. Always a fighter in a good cause, John Wayne exemplified the "muscular Jesus."

The generation born after World War II was raised on their

fathers' war stories and John Wayne movies. It is remarkable how often John Wayne is mentioned in the veterans' stories and in the literature that has grown out of the war. Truly, he was a cultural, national, and even a religious hero. John Wayne had come to portray and symbolize the link between what was right about America, its moral, even religious dimension, and its strength. For Jesus Christ to be truly believable, he had to deliver the way John Wayne did in the movies.

It is impossible to overestimate the impact the culture had on the Vietnam generation. They grew up in a country whose perceptions of war, particularly World War II, were of a great crusade, a battle between the forces of good and evil from which the righteous emerged victorious. American troops had been the agents of victory in the great crusade against the demonic foe. The American self-perception in 1945 was that of a people who had done God's work in the world through force of arms. We had been on "God's side." There was at that time no public doubt about the religious underpinning for what America did in the world.

The macho nature of the divine American mission exercised a powerful hold on the children of World War II veterans. Later they recognized this notion as a great seduction. One vet put it just that way: "I was seduced by World War II and John Wayne movies." But the Vietnam War, a test of manhood in good old John Wayne fashion, turned out to be a terribly cruel farce.

For the troops in Vietnam, war was supposed to be just as John Wayne portrayed it, not in the physical details of combat—the first firefight changed one's notions about that—but in the reason you fought. You fought only when the cause was just. It was necessary, right, and even good to fight on behalf of the weak and the downtrodden. The only way to meet aggression was with force. Deep down you knew that Jesus Christ endorsed John Wayne. After all, Jesus Christ Himself had to be a lot like John Wayne.

These attitudes cannot be attributed to childhood fantasies or adolescent daydreams. Rather, they arose from within the heart of American culture. They are deeply shared beliefs that impel our society to action in ways no other ideas can. The Vietnam generation was electrified by a magnificent young president who challenged them to "pay any price, bear any burden." Jesus Christ and John Wayne spoke through John F. Kennedy when he urged them to "Ask not what your country can do for you. Ask what you can do for your country."

Hundreds of thousands of young men and women accepted President Kennedy's challenge. They donned the uniform. Ron Kovic was one of them, and he was proud. He confided to his diary:

To be serving America in this its most critical hour, just like President Kennedy had talked about... It was very important to be there putting his life on the line, to be going out on patrol and lying in the rain for Sparky, the barber, and God and the rest. He was proud. He was real proud of what he was doing. This, he thought, is what serving your country is supposed to be about.[57]

The John Wayne and Jesus Christ connection amounts to a national myth. According to this myth, our nation is incapable of fighting an immoral war. The myth goes even further, in fact. Wars that we fight must not merely be just, but they must be waged in behalf of a holy cause. War must be a crusade. Our notion of war really doesn't derive from the just-war tradition in any way except in name. It is closer to the *jihad* (holy war) of Islam or to the Christian crusades against the Moslems in the eleventh and twelfth centuries—and these are now considered to be horrible, deeply sinful aberrations from Christian teaching and practice. In a holy war, the nasty business of killing is really God's work. Get on with it and God smiles on you.

We are not as far from the crusades in this country as we would like to think. During the early part of the Vietnam War, before the protests began, Christian ministers and church bodies endorsed the war with a crusade like intensity. Gloria Emerson gives us an example. In 1967, in a theology class in a small Catholic college, the priest-instructor was asked what he thought about the war in Vietnam. He replied, "If Christ were alive today, he would be a Marine carrying a rifle."[58] With this kind of endorsement, how is the average young student or soldier to distinguish the Redeemer from the Duke?

The Jesus Christ and John Wayne myth is pervasive. It lies at the heart of American self-definition as an article of religious faith.

GOD'S COUNTRY: THE CITY ON THE HILL

The intimacy between John Wayne and Jesus Christ is not something that sprang up after World War II just in time for a spate of movies to engrave it upon the memories of the Vietnam generation. It derives from a notion of divine destiny felt deeply by the first colonists who landed on the shores of an uncharted wilderness. Refugees from religious and political persecution in Europe, they saw their life on a new continent as much more than just another colonial settlement. Our pilgrim forebears felt that they had been called to a religious destiny unique in human history.

John Winthrop (1588-1649), who was to become the first governor of the Massachusetts Bay Colony, set a tone and direction to American life that remains almost unaltered to this day. Before disembarking in Salem Harbor in 1630, Winthrop reminded the settlers: "[We] must consider that we shall be as a City set upon a Hill, the [eyes] of all people are [upon] us."[59] In that moment the myth was born: America was to be a chosen people among the nations of the earth. It was to be a moral example to the rest of the world. The corollary was also implied by Winthrop: the rest of the world must keep its eyes upon us and follow our lead, for "the God of Israel is among us, when ten of us shall be able to resist a thousand of our enemies, when he shall make us a praise and glory..."[60]

The Lord's people, the colonists, believed they could depend on the God of Israel even in the face of overpowering odds. God is the true leader on whom the small settlement on the edge of a fearful wilderness was to rely. Their enemies were His enemies; their friends, His friends. From that day to this, whenever Americans have taken up the sword and gone into battle, they have carried with them their primal myth of origin. The myth survived the horror of black slavery, the extermination of the native peoples, Manifest Destiny, the Mexican War, and the war against Spain at the turn of this century.

The myth had its high moments. The American Revolution was an event often portrayed in terms of the Book of Exodus. Washington became in the eyes of his contemporaries—and of history—a Moses-like figure. A crisis that almost destroyed the nation became instead the event that verified the myth. The Civil War was transformed into a national religious sacrifice of self-purification. In the Civil War, as in the Revolution, force of arms carried the day. God vindicated His people, and the soldier was the agent who accomplished the divine purpose. Those willing to make the ultimate sacrifice in battle were then—and still are—accorded mythic status. Those who die in battle, like the fallen at Gettysburg in 1863, "shall not have died in vain." Lincoln, the martyred leader who brought us through the agony of civil war, became in death almost a Christ figure.

Woodrow Wilson, though he tried to "make the world safe for democracy" in World War I, could not impress the myth upon the rest of the world. World War II was a different matter. The "Crusade in Europe" and the defeat of the Japanese Empire were so complete and so stunning that the myth seemed finally verified beyond all doubt. America had indeed become the "the city on the hill."

The myth as it was transmitted to later generations of Americans remains incomplete, however. Winthrop and the Puritan colonists believed that the land and its people remained under the judgment of God. "Freedom," a word to which the American heart responds in a religious way, meant for the earliest Americans only a moral freedom "in reference to the covenant between God and man." It is a freedom to do "that only which is good, just and honest."[61] Lincoln, perhaps America's finest leader, had not lost the original religious underpinning of the myth. He assured the nation at his first inaugural that the nation stood under the judgment of God, that the war about to begin would exact for every drop of blood drawn by the slave master's lash a drop drawn by the sword.

During the late nineteenth and early twentieth centuries, the myth was thoroughly secularized, divorced from whatever connection with biblical religion it may have had originally. Though the notion of God and humankind's relationship to Him has been largely lost in the public culture, the myth of a chosen people and a city on the hill remains unabated.

Scholars call the mythology of a nation its "civil religion." Every tribe, people, and nation has some sort of civil religion. What distinguishes the American version from others is its dependence on the Hebrew and Christian Scriptures for its language and concepts. Though the United States owes its cultural origins as much to the philosophy, laws, and ideas of ancient Greece and Rome as it does to biblical religion, we have never acknowledged this fact. We prefer to express our self-understanding in terms of the traditional biblical faiths. Civil religion in America seems to resemble biblical religion, but in fact it is very different. The most significant areas of divergence between the two faiths lie in their respective notions of God and of the nature of humankind's relationship to him. This difference lies at the heart of the Vietnam veterans' problems with God.

Civil religion creates in America "a nation with the soul of a church."[62] Such a nation is convinced that transcendent goals lie at the heart of its own political processes. At the same time it inverts religion and constructs a model of God based on its own policy. Our political categories—law, justice, democracy, sovereignty—take on the characteristics of ultimate reality. The trouble with this is "when we relate American politics to God's sovereignty we also relate God's sovereignty to American politics."[63]

The face of the Great Seal of the United States expresses perfectly the religious nature of America. Its likeness is found on the reverse side of a dollar bill to the left of the motto "In God we trust." At the center of the Great Seal, one sees an unfinished pyramid, which represents the unfinished nature of the American undertaking. The top of the pyramid is formed by the all-seeing eye of God, who presides over the entire venture. The Latin words immediately over the eye of God proclaim: "He has presided over our beginnings." Inscribed in the base of the pyramid is the date 1776. The motto on the scroll under the pyramid is translated, "a new order of the ages." This new order does not refer merely to a new political beginning; rather, it points very clearly to a new religious and moral order. The human race has been made over in the American image, and God presides over this "new order of the ages."

The symbolism has diminished not at all over the centuries. The bitterness of the veterans derives from the failure of reality to match up to symbol. God did not deliver according to the promise of our most sacred national symbols and ideas. The "new order of the ages" could not be introduced into the provinces and villages of Vietnam. It was rejected at gunpoint, and God, ever the guarantor of the American way of life, was unable or unwilling to lead his people to victory over the infidels.

The continuing power of our pilgrim ancestors can never be overestimated. Even in a secular age when the public power of religion has been relegated to the fringes of culture, the notion that America lies at the center of the world's moral order is even stronger than it was in our national infancy.

Civil religion has long since become a national folk myth, influencing even the Christian churches that continue to take the biblical faith seriously. The sense of destiny at the root of the national myth is the "fatal flaw that opened the door to a self-righteousness and insensitivity of conscience that justified for some the rape of the American Indians, the development of the slave trade, and the philosophy of exploitive mercantilism."[64]

Like their Puritan ancestors, Americans are rigidly moralistic, concerned more with external behavior than with the moral and religious realities that lie deep within the human heart. We are concerned more with the "warm sins "—sexual indulgence, overeating, drinking—than we are with sins against justice such as war, the fostering of economic inequities, and the consequences of the unalloyed pursuit of material benefits.

Let us return once again to the soldier who questioned the balance between prostitution and "blowing away gooks" in the field. His religious upbringing had stressed illicit sex as certainly sinful, while it had endorsed his presence in a combat unit in Vietnam. Even though a Catholic, he was a legitimate son of his Puritan religious ancestors.

The ex-Marine with whom we began our story was unable to relate to a God who remained hidden in the corners of men's souls, one who did not rigidly enforce His will on either the enemy or the sinful hearts of His followers. Indeed, the killing went on in Vietnam, atrocities on both sides mounted, and God did not intervene to impose His will and bring about the outcome that divine destiny seemed to require. God did not perform as John Wayne would have done.

The Vietnam soldiers' dark night of the soul remained incomprehensible to them—and to the public—because the notions of God and religion, which we have all inherited as Americans, provide no means by which to interpret the experience. God simply didn't produce according to our expectations. He withheld from us in Vietnam the destiny promised those who shall inhabit the city on the hill.

After Vietnam, all Americans must question the meaning of our cultural folk religion, for the veterans proclaimed nothing less than the death of this national god.

"GOD WON'T LET ME ALONE"

Recognition of the moral question beyond "posttraumatic stress," belated though it may have been, was an especially significant step in the vets' pilgrimage back in the world. The moral issue requires its own resolution, but it also opens the door to the most perplexing and deeply disturbing of all the post-Vietnam questions:

Where was God in Vietnam? Where is He now?

The pandemic loss of religious faith among vets was, as we have seen, a direct result of Vietnam. This is a simple fact that cannot be explained away. Neither can it be treated as just another stress-related symptom. Because the "God question" relates to a person's ultimate meaning, it colors every other aspect of life. Is there any purpose to existence? Can there be any final personal destiny? Am I related to a creator and to all other beings, or am I merely floating aimlessly through a meaningless universe? These are questions as much alive today as ever in human history. We moderns are able to evade them to some extent because we have the technological resources to fill our minds with alluring distractions. We are also able to delude ourselves into believing that we have a measure of control over the elemental forces of destruction that so much absorbed our ancestors.

Vietnam vets, having personally faced these archetypal destructive forces, can no longer live comfortably in the world of delusion and distraction. The question of the absent God becomes more compelling as they approach the middle years of life. Having achieved some of the lesser goals they sought, having come face-to-face with the most serious moral questions of humanity, the vets now face once again the absent God who reappears in unexpected and often unwanted fashion.

The extent and power of God's re-emergence took the vets by surprise. One man complained, "I flipped God off after Vietnam, but he won't let me alone." Indeed, during the early 1980s God began to surface again among the vets from coast to coast. It seems that the early struggles back in the world consumed all available time an energy. God was written off in anger, and vets moved on to more immediate concerns.

As one who retained religious faith—though not unmixed with anger—I believed that the rejection of God was widespread and final. I had dealt with faith issues during the entire period I worked with vets. Though my function in the VA was a purely secular one (counselor-social worker-therapist), I was widely known as a former Army chaplain. Because of my background and willingness to listen, vets frequently discussed with me the moral and religious dislocation they had suffered. Many were willing to struggle with the moral dimensions of Vietnam despite the conventional wisdom that all was reducible to stress. The "God question" was another matter entirely. Though some men were on the road to rediscovering religious faith, my impression was that most had slammed the door on the religious option.

I was quite surprised to begin receiving phone calls from vet counselors across the country during 1981 and 1982 asking for advice on how to deal with God's re-emergence in the veteran consciousness. At about the same time, I was asked to conduct training seminars for VA mental health professionals and Vet

Center counselors on the moral and religious dilemmas of Vietnam vets. The seminars, which always include consultation with vets themselves, have continued through the present time. I conducted some of these training sessions in conjunction with Walter Capps, a University of California religious studies scholar,[65] and others I did alone.

The God question comes up in a variety of ways in the seminars and in individual sessions. Some vets have pursued their religious quest in Jungian directions; others have taken up Eastern religions and philosophies. Most former Christians, however, yearn for some contact with the God they "flipped off" in Vietnam. They want to interpret their experience in Christian terms. These vets have demanded of me a perspective and a frame of reference from which to cope with a troublesome God who seemed at one point to have abandoned them but who now intrudes again into their lives. What follows is an outline of this perspective.

DON'T LET GOD OFF THE HOOK

"Flipping off" God, screaming at Him, "Where were you?" and feeling spiritually alienated are appropriate religious reactions to Vietnam. Some of the words and gestures used by vets to express their feelings about God may be deficient in good taste, but the issue is not one of social grace. The point is that the Vietnam religious experience merits a powerful response. If God was AWOL in Vietnam, He should be cited for dereliction of duty. If, on the other hand, God was running a "clandestine operation" of His own in the jungles of Southeast Asia, then perhaps He will reveal something about it when pressed to do so.

My own problem with God surfaced when I was unable to address God as "Abba" in prayer. "Abba" is the word used by

Jesus to address the Father. It is a colloquialism, the Aramaic equivalent of "Daddy," and expresses the Christian relationship with God. For several years after Vietnam I was simply unable to use this word in my own conversations with God, because daddies don't do things like this to their children. My question of God is "How are you really Abba?"

Though our culture equates religion with sugar and good feelings, there is much biblical precedent for a more boisterous relationship with God: Jacob wrestled with the angle; Moses argued with God throughout his entire career; Jeremiah tried to get out of doing what God wanted; Jonah and Balaam went off in other directions when God gave them their orders. Simon Peter argued with Jesus. James and John made unreasonable demands on Him. Saul of Tarsus began his journey to the Christian faith by persecuting its adherents.

Contemporary religious people also struggle with God. The story is told of the rabbi who was late for services in the synagogue. The cantor went to his office and was about to knock on the door when he heard shouting from inside. He knocked tentatively. When the door was opened, he asked the rabbi what had happened. The rabbi replied, "I was speaking to God."

An old monk, terminally ill, was talking with members of his community around his bedside. They began to tease him—as monks will—about his rapidly approaching death. One of them said, "Brother, you will soon be facing God, and you will have a lot to answer for to Him." The dying monk replied, "And He will have a lot to answer for to me."

Authentic biblical religion allows for a vigorous dialogue with God. It should come as no surprise, however, that God's end of the dialogue should be at least as powerful as the challenge hurled at him. Having been "flipped off," screamed at, and forcibly ejected from one's life, God may simply refuse to stay away. None of us—least of all myself—should have been surprised that "God won't let me alone."

JOB'S QUESTION—BUT WE'RE NOT JOB!

The question asked at the very beginning of this book, Where was God in Vietnam? demands an answer. Any suggestion that a vet could reestablish contact with God apart from this central issue would amount to repetition of the familiar "chaplain bull-shit."

We must recognize, however, that the question has been asked before, and we must examine its ancient formulation. The Hebrew Scripture (what Christians call the Old Testament) raises the "Vietnam question" in the Book of Job.

If there is any religious experience that Vietnam vets can relate to it is surely Job's. More than any other Christian image, that of Christ on the cross speaks to vets. Who of us cannot cry out with him: "My God, my God, why have you forsaken me?"

For anyone who takes Vietnam seriously in a religious sense, Job's question is the only one worth asking and the experience of Christ abandoned on the cross is all that is personally relevant. All other religious considerations "don't mean nothin'."

Job lost his family and all his possessions. He was afflicted with sickness and sores. He suffered so much that he cursed the day he was born. When his friends came to comfort him, they were horrified by what they found. They insisted that Job must have sinned to deserve this kind of suffering from the hand of God, but Job protested his innocence. The friends persisted. Job must be guilty of sin, or else his suffering makes no sense. The friends made the connection between sin and suffering: God uses suffering as a correction for sin. In their minds, everyone who suffers does so because of sin. They also reminded Job that his material prosperity was a sign of his innocence. Loss of his possessions was proof that his suffering was a just punishment for sin. Job's friends insisted that his protests of innocence could not be true, otherwise God is at fault for allowing punishment to befall the innocent.

Job would not yield. He insisted he had done nothing to deserve what happened to him. Even God Himself attested to Job's innocence. Job could make no sense of his suffering. His experience contradicted what he understood of God from the Scriptures and traditions of his own people. The God of Israel was on the side of the poor and suffering. He led his people out of slavery. God defended those deprived of justice. These were the beliefs and traditions of Israel, but God's treatment of Job is more like that of a capricious and evil tyrant. Since God allows the same fate to befall both the innocent and the guilty, perhaps there is no such thing as divine justice. If God is good and at the same time powerful, why is his justice so ineffective in the world? Why doesn't God bring about the good that He wills and remove the evil that supposedly thwarts His designs? These were Job's questions.

Job pursues his "Vietnam question" relentlessly. He exhausts all other possible answers and finds them unsatisfactory. Job anguishes not merely because of his physical sufferings, though these are terrible. He is even more deeply troubled by his own dark night of the soul, for now he no longer comprehends God. Everything he thought and believed about God is called into question. But Job persists, and finally he forces God to answer.

Vietnam vets can relate to Job's experience, to his bleakness of soul and to his question, but we do not stand in the same position with respect to God as he did, for Job was truly innocent. Before we continue to press God for an answer as Job did, we should look more carefully at the matter of our own innocence. We will return to Job's question later, but we must first explore an avenue that Job's friends proposed. Perhaps there is, in our case, a connection between suffering and sin.

GOD CHECKED OUT OF VIETNAM BECAUSE OF WHAT WAS GOIN' DOWN

In a discussion following one of my seminars, a vet suggested one reason for God's absence in Vietnam. "God checked out of 'Nam because of what was goin' down there." He further observed, "I would've checked out, too, if I could've."

The vet's observation is theologically profound. Job's friends had part of the picture right—there is a connection between sin and suffering. One of the key points of biblical faith is that God created humankind with free will. Adam and Eve, though graced by God, sinned. Cain killed Abel. From its beginnings, the human condition is marked by sin. The possibility of sin, turning against God and our fellow creatures— missing the mark of life's purpose—is one inalterable consequence of human freedom. In fact, humanity does misuse its freedom with terrifying consistency and with horrible results. God's response to sin lies not in removing human freedom but in allowing it full scope. Ultimate justice, the vindication of divine goodness, and redemption from evil transcend, but in no way contravene, the human capacity for autonomous action.

God makes room for sin within the boundaries of humanity. He also grants to humankind glimpses and glimmers of His caring presence. But the act of sinning excludes the sense of God's protective presence. One cannot be immersed in sin and at the same time expect to feel the loving presence of God. Adam and Eve felt naked after sinning and tried to hide from God. Sin necessarily includes some awareness of our own nakedness and of our distance from God. God indeed "checked out" of our lives in Vietnam because we "checked out" on Him.

Former Chaplain Gaylen Meyer writes: "The jungles of Vietnam revealed that we Americans are hollow people.... If a man is hollow, spiritually and morally hollow, there is nothing inside of him to restrain his behavior."[66] Meyer describes what happens to the hollow man in combat: "Because of the vacuum in his soul, the powers of darkness fill him and he embraces them."[67]

That is a pretty good description of the sin of war, not just for Americans but for anyone. One cannot embrace both God and the powers of darkness simultaneously. The first step in resuming the dialogue with God is to make no protest of innocence but to admit that we have been swallowed up by the sin of war. We may then legitimately demand of God some answers, as did Job, but only after we have confronted the reality of war as sin and faced up to the fact that we ourselves were participants in sin.

The notion of war as sin simply doesn't play in Peoria—or anywhere else in the United States—because a fondness for war is an essential component of the macho American god. We define deity as that supreme being who achieves his ends by force. In our cultural definition of God, his divine purposes and our national goals are coextensive. The nation is the agent by which God works His will in the world. The means by which these purposes are realized is force. Given these assumptions, it is extraordinarily difficult to conduct a public discussion of war sin. Yet the awareness of evil—in religious terms a consciousness of sin—is the underlying motif of the Vietnam War stories.

If the Vietnam narratives demonstrate an awareness of sin on the part of the vets, then the "back in the world" stories depict a consciousness of a further and even more heinous sin on the part of those who scapegoated them: hypocrisy. Both vets and their accusers must be placed within a biblical frame of reference.

He then spoke this parable addressed to those who believed in their own self-righteousness while holding everyone else in contempt:

Two men went up to the temple to pray: one was a Pharisee, the other a tax collector. The Pharisee with head unbowed prayed in this fashion: "I give you thanks, O God, That I am not like the rest of men— grasping, crooked, adulterous—or even like this tax collector. I fast twice a week. I pay tithes on all I possess." The other man, however, kept his distance, not even daring to raise his eyes to heaven. All he did was beat his breast and say "0 God, be merciful to me, a sinner." Believe me, this man went home from the temple justified but the other did not. For everyone who exalts himself shall be humbled while he who humbles himself shall be exalted. [Luke 18:10-14]

If Gaylen Meyer is correct and we showed ourselves to be hollow people in Vietnam, then it is also true that no one knows this better than the vets. We at least know and have made some admission of our hollowness, while the rest of the country remains self-righteous, smug, and morally shallow with respect to real sins like war.

I believe the implicit acknowledgment of sin—which is what the war stories are all about—is much closer to the kind of humility mentioned by Jesus in the parable than most of what passes for virtue in America. Perhaps Vietnam vets—angry at God, confused by evil of an immense magnitude, walking in unaccustomed darkness—are actually very close to the kind of spiritual emptiness that God fills with His gracious presence. As the parable reminds us, there is no room for God in those who are puffed up with self-righteousness.

If this is true, the emptiness must be filled by God and not by a popular substitute for God.

«« —»»

GOD WAS NOT IN THE MARINES

Despite the priest/teacher mentioned by Gloria Emerson, who believed that had Christ come in 1968, he would have been in the Marines, all the biblical evidence indicates otherwise. The step we must take in approaching God once more is to rid ourselves of the lethal religious baggage we carry around in the form of American civil religion, the John Wayne and Jesus Christ model of God.

Gaylen Meyer is both eloquent and accurate:

> As a nation too we took a painful trip inside ourselves through the Vietnam war. When we finally saw into our heart of darkness, we discovered the bankruptcy of American civil religion. We found that God is not necessarily on our side—and that American military action could be nothing more than a plain, brutal war in spite of our desire to see it as a righteous crusade with some transcendent purpose to justify the violence. We learned that the Kingdom of God was yet to come—and that we were not it in spite of our Puritan beginnings as a "city set upon a hill." Most of all, we learned that our long-held sense of innocence was a sham...[68]

Civil religion remains a powerful and popular form of idolatry. Inveighing against the alluring idea that we as a nation are the "new order of the ages" does nothing to destroy the belief. For that we must confront the God who emerges in the history of Israel and who finally comes among us in the person of Christ. Here again we return to Scripture.

THE BURNING BUSH

When Moses was tending his flock at Horeb, God spoke to him from the middle of a burning bush that was not consumed in the fire. God told him to take off his shoes for the place was holy ground. Moses "hid his face for he was afraid to look at God." (Exod. 3:6) The message was clear: God and Moses were not on the same level. Moses understood that "the God of Abraham, the God of Isaac and the God of Jacob" was totally beyond him. God in the Hebrew Scriptures is the one who calls everything into being out of nothingness and who holds the universe in the "span of his hand." The only appropriate responses to God are worship and obedience.

Though God becomes intimate with his people, defends them, cares for them, and makes a bargain with them, He remains essentially inaccessible. Moses discovered this when God disclosed that He would do what Moses asked "because you have found favor with me and you are my intimate friend." (Exod. 33:17) Moses, emboldened by his intimacy with God, asked, "Do let me see your glory," which amounted to a request to know God face-to-face, almost as an equal. God explained that "my face you cannot see, for no man sees me and still lives." But God promised Moses that He would place him in a cleft of a rock, shield his face, and "you may see my back; but my face is not to be seen." (Exod. 33:18-23) No more than Moses can we fathom God face-to-face understand Him as He really is. The glimpses we get of God in this life are always of his "backside."

It is important to remember this, because all idolatries are attempts to fashion a god with whom we are more comfortable, one who can be understood and even manipulated. The people of Israel became impatient and frightened while Moses was on the mountaintop and fashioned a golden calf, a god they could control. American civil religion is also an idol. Unlike ancient idols, this one purports to be identical with the God revealed in Scripture. At least the people of Israel were honest about it. They got tired of waiting and more than a little frightened, so they made themselves what they knew was a substitute for God. They didn't pretend it was the real God as we do. It might be argued that the New Testament renders God more accessible and intimate. It is true that God becomes physically intimate with humanity in the person of Christ, revealing far more about himself than he did in the covenant with Israel. At the same time, the New Testament makes it quite clear that we are dealing with the same transcendent and "totally other" God who placed Moses in the cleft of the rock.

The prologue of John's Gospel proclaims that "the Word became flesh and made his dwelling among us." At the same time, the Gospel insists that the same Word existed "in the beginning." "The Word was in God's presence and the Word was God." (John 1) Paul tells us, "He is the image of the invisible God and the first-born of all creatures. In him everything in heaven and on earth was created." (Col. 1:15-16) Even though He is now physically intimate with humankind, the Word made flesh remains the "totally other" God.

The same notion is found in the Gospel accounts of Jesus' relationships with his followers. Though the disciples became "no longer servants but friends" of Jesus, they nonetheless knew Him as the Master. After the resurrection, they were uneasy, though comforted in His presence. The two disciples on the road to Emmaus were awestruck when they recognized the risen Lord in the breaking of the bread. Mary Magdalene, one of his closest friends, was told by the risen Jesus, "Do not touch me for I have not yet ascended to the Father." When confronted by the risen Lord, whom he had doubted, Thomas simply said, "My Lord and my God." The New Testament reveals the same transcendent and essentially inaccessible God, who now deals with humankind in a new, intimate, and unexpected way.

American civil religion diminishes, reduces, and ultimately destroys the transcendence of God even though it continues to employ the biblical language of the Hebrew Scripture. Fortunately, our form of civil religion has never made any pretense of constructing an idolatrous image of the intimacy of God revealed in the New Testament.

The biblical God remains a God of mystery, not of manageability. In Vietnam, God could not be persuaded to stop the Vietcong atrocities against the Vietnamese or their relentless killing of American soldiers. The North Vietnamese Army, despite the fact that they were an arm of an explicitly atheistic system of government, continued to pour into South Vietnam, inflicting heavy losses on our own people. We couldn't get a handle on God to have him halt the influx of the "heathen horde."

Much more to the point, God did nothing to slow the descent of American troops into the barbarism and brutality of war. He allowed men who believed in him to taste fully the savagery and ferocity of killing. Despite the increasing loss of faith and the anger against him, God continued to allow Christian troops to slaughter the innocent, inflicting the suffering of Job upon others. Evil is, on some levels, almost a transcendent reality, far more, apparently, than the sum of all its parts. Evil on this scale becomes unmanageable, itself a mystery that can be neither explained nor articulated.

God allowed teenaged soldiers, a random selection of American youth, to live out the story in the Book of Genesis. They ate of the tree of the knowledge of good and evil. As a consequence, they were expelled from the garden of innocence. For most Americans, the story is a platitude; for vets, it is a personal experience. The real question is not why it happened in Vietnam but why it happens at all.

When asking any question about God, we must always return to the story of the burning bush. God simply revealed himself without explanation to Moses as "I am who I am." God shows himself as one who imposes his will upon humankind and upon history. He alone creates all that is. He alone saves and judges. His domain is as wide as all reality.

Among monks and mystics, it is commonly understood that we know more what God is not than what He is. They know that all religious language is inadequate, for God simply cannot be comprehended. Even when we say that God exists or that God is good, we must remember that even these commonly understood words do not apply to God in the same way they apply to anything else. God is always known obscurely. He is always perceived amidst a "cloud of unknowing."

For the mystics, God cannot be explained or comprehended, but He can be experienced in the depths of one's soul in a profound way that defies articulation. In this experience, God becomes more real than anyone or anything else. He draws a person deeper into the transcendent mystery of his own being. This experience of God always entails a passage through what the mystics call "the dark night of the soul." To undergo this kind of union with God, one must first be emptied of self through a painful and very bleak process. At the end, one is left speechless and empty and yet filled with the magnificence of God's presence.

The experience of the mystics is the biblical experience lived to its fullest extent. I believe this most profound religious experience is now available to the Vietnam soldiers who "flipped off" God. Which brings us back to Job.

BACK TO JOB

Job demands an answer of God. He wants to know whether God is believable. He also wants to know where he stands with God. He complains, "I cry to you but you do not answer me; you stand off and look at me." (30:20) And again: "This is my final plea; let the Almighty answer me!" (31:37)

God *does* answer. The answer is not to the question of why the innocent Job is suffering. Rather, God addresses the other points raised by Job: Who is God, what is he doing in the world, and what is humankind's relationship to him?

God's reply touches Job in a way he had not expected.

> Where were you when I founded the earth? Tell me, if you have understanding. Who determined its size; do you know? Who stretched out the measuring line for it? Into what were its pedestals sunk, and who laid the cornerstone, While the morning stars sang in chorus and all the sons of God shouted for joy. And who shut within doors the sea, when it burst forth from the womb; When I made the clouds its garment and thick darkness its swaddling bands? When I set limits for it and fastened the bar of its door, And said: Thus far shall you come but no farther, and here shall your proud waves be stilled!
> (Job 38:4-11)

When he understands God's reply, Job reaches a new level of religious awareness. His question about innocent suffering and God's will remains unanswered, but Job completes his journey out of the night. His soul is finally at rest, and he replies to God.

> Behold, I am of little account; what can I answer you? I put my hand over my mouth. Though I have spoken once, I will not do so again; though twice, I will do so no more.
> (Job 40:4-5)

Job, his question still unanswered, arrives at a new awareness of who God is. Like Moses, Isaiah, Jeremiah, and the New Testament disciples who confronted the risen Lord, Job enters in a new way into the presence of the all-powerful God. Even from the depths of his own suffering Job understands that humanity cannot comprehend God's mind or fathom his purposes. He is humbled by his new experience of God. He says:

> I know that you can do all things and that no purpose of yours can be hindered. I have dealt with great things that I do not understand; things too wonderful for me, which I cannot know. I heard of you by word of mouth, but now my eye has seen you. Therefore, I disown what I have said, and repent in dust and ashes.
> (Job: 42:2-6)

Perhaps the best the human mind can do in dealing with Job's question is to recognize that real freedom of will necessarily entails the possibility of sin. In Vietnam, human freedom led to sin on a massive scale. In combat the randomness of death was incomprehensible. Would we still be human if it were otherwise? Before this question the mind surrenders. We come back again to Job.

The answer which Job receives is not in the form of words but in the form of an experience, that is, a realization of creaturely existence in the presence of the Creator. It is not the time for questions but for faith and humility. Job comes to the stage where his original question of why he is suffering in spite of being innocent becomes irrelevant. He has been transformed and, in the context of his changed state, that question slips into obscurity. He has learned that "the beginning of wisdom is the fear of the Lord." Thus he withdraws his question because he has grasped that he is a creature and his destiny is well protected by this mysterious God who demands complete surrender on Job's part.

Those who ask the "Vietnam question" with such intensity and depth are at least potentially open to Job's answer.

MY GOD, MY GOD...

American public religion has been largely filtered through the Christian prism. Most vets I've met who struggled with their faith in Vietnam had been members of a Christian congregation. For them as for all Christians, the religious focus is upon Jesus of Nazareth.

Christians believe that the God so far above us, so beyond our powers of intellect and imagination, finally bridged the distance between Himself and us in a marvelous way. He became physical with us. He slipped quietly, unobtrusively, into our history and into our personal lives. Now we could know Him and grasp Him in the only way we can—physically.

The images of God stamped by Jesus upon humanity are those of weakness, even of fragility. A stable in a cave for a birthplace, special friendship with the poor and out-casts, insistence on love—even of enemies—the paradoxes in the Sermon on the Mount, all subvert conventional wisdom and our self-assurances about the way things are.

No Christian image is more subversive or troublesome than the cross. When Jesus confronted evil, He lost. When He faced sin, it overcame Him. Though He desired to be spared suffering, He was not. Like all of us, He protested the approach of death, but even He yielded before it. The message given to us in a physical way in the flesh of Jesus is a most disturbing one.

The worst of it is that Jesus, too, underwent not just the physical agony of crucifixion but spiritual anguish as well. The primordial "dark night" experience was His. When death approached, Jesus cried out, making His own the words of the psalmist, "My God, my God, why have you forsaken me?"

(Mark 15:34) Even the consolation given to Job at the end was denied to Jesus. If it is true that "the servant is not greater than the Master" and that faith calls upon us to take up your cross and follow me, then we are indeed in the hands of a God whose ways are completely incomprehensible.

The final words spoken by Jesus as recorded in Luke's Gospel (Luke 23:46) are these: "Father, into your hands I commend my spirit." Having passed through the ultimate desolation of his spirit, Jesus placed himself in the hands of the Father. Then He died.

The "newness of life in Christ," the power of the risen Lord and the hope He gives to all of us, and the transformation of the disciples in the Spirit occur only as a result of the cross. Easter comes after Good Friday not just for Jesus but for his followers, as well. The risen Lord is God's answer to humanity's most disturbing question. God alone is able to transform life, death, sin, suffering—and all meaning—so totally. Before this God our most profound and anguished questions are but prelude to his presence.

Paradoxically, the journey out of the night requires that one first enter into the darkest regions of the spirit. Somehow, making the transition from Job's question and Jesus' cry of anguish into that state of soul where one can say with Christ, "Father, into your hands I commend my spirit" is the crucial step. In that moment and in that spiritual condition, one is grasped at last by a transcendent brightness.

CHAPTER SIX:
WHAT IT ALL MEANS

The Vietnam War produced social, political, and economic ramifications that will be felt for decades. What all this ultimately means for the American people and for the world will unfold only gradually. For this reason, it may not be obvious immediately that the Vietnam experience has significance except as a spiritual odyssey for anyone but the vets themselves. It is a pilgrimage important for all of us, however, and the reason is clear: political discourse in our country never escapes national religious and moral underpinnings. This is true even though we make much of the separation between church and state. America is, after all, convinced it is "the nation with the soul of a church."

The nation is not a church, however, and therein lies the problem. Its foreign policy, especially decisions regarding the use of military force, would be conceived far differently if we Americans were to relinquish our claim to special religious status and become, in our own minds, a mere nation among other nations. If we are ever to understand this distinction, the Church—the real one—must truly separate itself from the nation-church. The real Church must publicly reclaim its hold on Scripture and interpret the spiritual journeys of warriors and a warring people according to the revelation that has been entrusted not to the nation but to the Church.

The Vietnam religious experience takes on immense importance to the Church, which, like it or not, must confront Vietnam and the veterans. The vets did not arrive in Southeast Asia from another planet. They came from the American heartland. The Christian faith that crumbled in the moral wilderness of Vietnam was a faith engendered and nourished within the Church. Vietnam is a mirror in which the American community can see itself. The reflection is not what we would like to see, but our own faith compels us to look carefully at the image.

The word *Church,* as I understand it, is inclusive. It refers not to Roman Catholicism, Protestantism, Anglicanism, or Eastern Orthodox as separate entities but to the entire Body of Christ—all of us together. We who profess faith in Jesus Christ and are baptized into the community that bears His name are stuck with each other. Denominational divisions within Christianity arose because differing but authentic interpretations of the Gospel were linked with political conflict. The underlying unity of the Church has often been obscured by petty nationalism and by the institutional inertia of the various branches of Christianity, but our unity remains rooted in Christ despite our attempts to subvert His command that we "all may be one."

The Vietnam religious question poses a challenge to the Church at the center of its spiritual life. Unless the Church returns to the cross of Christ—where its unity begins—it cannot even understand the Vietnam question, much less respond to it. In the shadow of the cross, denominational differences are as meaningless as are national and political identities. No branch of the Church may inoculate itself against Vietnam; the entire Body has been invaded.

Vietnam is all about the cross: death, despair, and sin. Those who have been touched by Vietnam understand the cross and cry out for new life, hope, forgiveness, and the promise of the risen Lord. These are also the central issues of the Christian faith, and they render all other religious questions insignificant. We cannot grapple with these issues unless we go beyond both the idolatry of American civil religion and the seemingly endless trivial differences between various Christian denominations. When we come to grips with Vietnam, we also encounter Christ crucified and risen. The vets' experience thus confronts civil religion and poses a direct challenge to the shallow spiritual life of much of American Christianity.

Often, when I have discussed the Vietnam religious experience with fellow Christians who did not serve there, I am reminded that we are Americans and must continue to love our country. This response—typical of many American Christians, I fear—demonstrates a failure to distinguish between religion and patriotism. The difference is crucial.

Members of the Church may indeed be patriotic Americans, but patriotism is not the concern of the Church. Patriotism is a civic virtue, a morally good quality; it is not the business of the Church, however. The Church is called to live and proclaim the Gospel of Jesus Christ. It is called to observe the commandments of both the Hebrew and Christian covenants. Tragically, we American Christians have allowed our patriotism and our religious faith to intermingle. We have allowed a national folklore to acquire the status of revealed truth. Our historical failure to distinguish between the two has led us to tolerate, and even worse, to perpetrate violence in the name of this religion.

Every nation, of course, has symbols and images that exert a powerful influence on its citizens. This is an inescapable, necessary, and healthy part of national life. It is the foundation of patriotism, which is a civic virtue. Patriotism remains a virtue for Americans as well as for other peoples in the world. Our nation has produced a government and a way of life as fine as any the world has ever known, and we have a right to be proud of our country. The American historical experience was—and still is—magnificent and exhilarating. But patriotism is not the same thing as religion—at least not within the context of the Christian understanding of religion.

The vets, together with the Church that nourished them, have become trapped in a very ancient way of looking at the world-mythology. The journey out of the spiritual night is very much a release from that entanglement and a return to an authentic biblical faith.

GOD OF SCRIPTURE, GODS OF MYTH

Earlier in the book, we discussed American civil religion, referring to it as myth and distinguishing between it and biblical religion. It is important to understand something about myths and how these relate to biblical narrative.

Part of the distinction between civil religion and biblical religion lies in the nature of mythology itself. The word *myth* comes from the Greek *mythos,* which means story. Myth is not a fictional account of an event but a symbolic expression of reality. Myth presents in symbolic form

> the unknown transcendental reality which lies beyond observation and simple deduction, but which is recognized as existing and operative... The mythic form is always symbolic of the reality which it apprehends obscurely and only through an intuition.[70]

Mythmaking is a universal human phenomenon. Ancient peoples understood the origins of the world and of their own societies in mythic terms. The evolution of philosophy and the development of science have provided the tools for logical analysis of reality and more satisfactory explanations of the physical processes of nature. Despite the successes of philosophy and science, however, myth continues to provide an insight into ultimate reality "more profound than scientific description and logical analysis can ever achieve."[71]

Myth remains in the modern world. Science itself develops its own mythology, and nations continue to view themselves in mythic terms. The Soviet state furnishes an example of this: it continues to operate on the mythological assumptions of Karl Marx with respect to the final outcome of human history.

Scripture often uses symbolic and mythic forms of expression because these are the only terms that seem to comprehend and articulate ultimate reality. The difference between Scripture and the ancient myths lies in the notion of God. The biblical understanding of God does not arise from some intuition into the nature of reality, as do the ancient myths, but from a personal experience, an encounter. Abraham, Moses, the prophets, the people of Israel, the disciples of Jesus, Peter, James, John, and Paul, the first generation of the Christian church—all experienced the intrusion of the transcendent God into their own lives and into the world. God, the unknown reality, is now partially known to them because He has revealed himself. Mythic thought and language in Scripture are always shaped by the personal experience of God—not the other way around, as is the case in ancient pagan myths.

The gods of the myths are expressions of the peoples' intuition into the nature of reality. The gods take on the characteristics of the seasonal cycle, of the forces of nature, and of the tribe itself. Ancient mythologies describe events in a world other than that of ordinary human experience. They deal with the endless cycle of the cosmos and of nature. The story is simply told as a description of some mysterious reality. However valid the ancient intuitions might be, they are not, and do not claim to be, the personal revelation of the transcendent God.

The Hebrew Scriptures make just such a claim: God speaks, reveals, and acts in history. Once He is known through revelation of Himself in a personal encounter, symbolic language must be used to express the experience, because no other language is adequate. At the same time, even symbolic language is really inadequate; it is simply the best we have. No mental images or language patterns, even those of Scripture, can truly capture and convey the reality of God.

Authentic biblical religion never forgets that God cannot be seen "face-to-face." When we bargain with God as Moses did, we still see only His "backside." When we push Him for an explanation as Job did, we receive Job's answer. When we confront the risen Lord as Thomas did, we are reduced to a simple confession: "My Lord and my God." The God revealed in Scripture resists any attempt to reduce him to smaller and more manageable proportions.

A second characteristic distinguishes myth from Scripture. Unlike mythology, Scripture contains an ethical emphasis, a moral imperative intimately connected with revelation. God makes demands of His people. This is not true in mythology. A comparison of two stories, one from mythology and the other from Scripture, in which one brother kills another, demonstrates the difference.[72]

The tale of Romulus and Remus is the foundational story of Rome. Twin brothers, raised by a wolf, return as adults to human society. They decide to build a city but quarrel over its exact location. Romulus begins building, but Remus ridicules him. Romulus becomes angry and kills Remus. He then becomes the first citizen and soldier of Rome. No moral guilt attaches to the killing of his brother, and no punishment befalls him.

In the biblical story, Cain becomes jealous of his brother Abel because God seems to favor Abel. Cain takes his brother into a field, attacks and kills him. Unlike Romulus, Cain does not escape the consequences of his brother's murder, for God asks him, "Where is your brother, Abel?" Cain denies knowledge of his brother's whereabouts, asking God, "Am I my brother's keeper?" God assures Cain, "Your brother's blood cries out to me from the soil!" God then punishes Cain for his crime. (Gen. 4:8-16)

Not only does mythology make no ethical demands; it frequently masks moral evil. Myth describes human reality, much of which is evil. By acting out the myth, one simply participates in the grand scenario of the way things are. Israel's God, on the other hand, is concerned with the moral dimension of human activity and holds His people accountable for their conduct.

Moral accountability grew out of God's covenant with Israel, but the primary responsibility of the people was to remain faithful to God. Above all, they were to remain faithful to Him, not only by observing His commands but by keeping Him in their hearts and minds before all else. They were to worship Him alone. No other god, image, or idol was to be placed before Him.

The authors of the Hebrew Scriptures believed that the gods who peopled the myths of their contemporaries were not gods at all. Other tribes represented their deities with statues and images, but the Israelites considered these to be "graven images," meaningless idols. Yet their own besetting temptation and most frequent sins were idolatry and infidelity to God. Above all else, Israel was commanded to avoid entanglement in the mythologies of its contemporaries. They often failed, but they always returned to God.

Their first failure was the classic and most easily remembered example. While the people awaited the return of Moses from Mount Sinai, they became impatient with him—and with God—so they fashioned their own idol, a god with whom they could be more comfortable—a graven image. By doing this, they violated the first and most important commandment given to them by God: the first commandment.

I, the LORD, am your God, who brought you out of the land of Egypt, that place of slavery. You shall not have other gods besides me. You shall not carve idols for yourselves in the shape of anything in the sky above or on the earth below or in the waters beneath the earth: you shall not bow down before them or worship them. (Exod. 20:2-5a)

The commandment remains a cornerstone of the Christian community, as well. In fact, Jesus was no less clear when He gave us the two commandments of the new covenant. The first one was: "You shall love the Lord your God with all your heart, with all your soul, with all your strength and with all your mind." (Luke 10:27)

The biblical lesson is clear. When they become absolutes, when they are placed before the true God, mythologies become idolatrous.

OUR COUNTRY'S MYTH

The American myth diverges from Scripture in much the same way as do the ancient mythologies. American civil religion, like ancient mythology, constructs a god based on its own intuition of reality. An exuberant people, facing an uncharted wilderness and hostile tribes, improving immensely the political structures they had inherited, saw themselves as a beacon to the world. The "new order of the ages" was simply a mythological description of the way things were in 1776 and would forever remain.

Early Americans did not, of course, express their beliefs by telling stories about gods creating a new people out of the political chaos in the world. Such a device would have been too naive for the seventeenth and eighteenth centuries. The spirit of that period was an extreme rationalism and viewed God as a supreme but aloof architect who created the universe and then governed it from afar. It would have been unacceptable for another reason as well. Most of the colonists were Christians who would have rejected any obvious supplanting of Scripture.

American mythology never explicitly intended to rewrite either the Hebrew or Christian Scripture, but the enthusiasm for the emerging nation was so great that the public culture implicitly assumed that the promises made to Israel by God thousands of years before were now fulfilled in a later age by America. The image of the god who presided over this new age was drawn from popular notions about God current among enlightened Americans of the time.

American civil religion is a true mythology because it rests upon an intuition of transcendent reality, in this case, the fulfillment of the world's political order eternally willed by God. It eviscerates the image of God found in the religious traditions of both synagogue and church, leaving only a sterile and remote "providence" who presides over the new political order in the world. America occupies the central position in the new age, as Israel did among the ancient peoples.

As we have seen, American civil religion disguises itself by appropriating biblical symbols and imagery. Vietnam revealed the most arrogant feature of the masquerade the assumption of divine power with respect to the rest of the world. The irony of Vietnam is that it unmasked the myth by revealing the moral ugliness of war and afflicting the warriors with spiritual pain.

Vietnam soldiers went into battle under cover of the myth. Killing was to be as painless for them as it had been for John Wayne—or for Romulus—but the mythology could not shelter them from the demands of biblical faith. The dead turned out to be not the harmless corpse of Remus but their brother Abel. Spilled blood cried out from the ground, and God demanded an accounting. The religious paradox of Vietnam was certainly this: American teenagers, sheltered by a myth that masks the evil of war, rediscovered the biblical God because they came to realize that His commands were to be taken seriously.

American mythological intuition proved itself hollow on the battlefields of Vietnam. The "divine providence" that presided over our national origins and still supposedly guides our efforts and that makes no demands on us—the god in whose name the soldiers fought—was indeed absent from the field. In his place stood the God who judges human acts and who destroys the graven images inscribed on the mind as well as those carved out of metal. The aloof abstraction of American mythology—"divine providence"—cannot reduce one's life to such a shambles that its meaning can be expressed only in a cry of nihilism: "It don't mean nothin'." But the God described in the pages of Scripture has this kind of power. He destroys all our petty certainties, working in the midst of chaos and even from within the emptiness of human sin. He operated this way among the vets, whose religious experience became, quite unexpectedly, a biblical one.

The paradox is complete. An experience that results in the loss of religious faith among veterans seems antithetical in every way to what the Bible is all about. Does God not, after all work in the soul to enhance the awareness of His presence? Does not the God of the Bible lead His followers on to an ever deeper knowledge of Himself? The answer to these two questions is certainly yes but the God of the Bible usually appears in places and in situations where He is least expected, and He works in ways that are entirely incomprehensible. I believe the Vietnam dark night of the spirit, with all its bitterness and loss of faith among vets, is just such an authentic biblical religious experience. It is totally unexpected and largely incomprehensible to Americans because it contradicts the prevailing religious experience and expectations of our culture. It is this cultural experience—not that of the vets—that is largely mythological and bogus by biblical standards. The one agency able to understand the vets' spiritual journey in darkness and then interpret its meaning publicly is the Church, but the Church has been shamefully silent and hopelessly inept in this regard. I believe the reason for this failure is clear. The Church has allowed itself to be influenced by the mythology.

THE VETS AND THE CHURCH

Vietnam vets, most of whom are unschooled in theology and uninterested in church matters, are nonetheless able to relate to Christian faith at its deepest levels. Job's question, Jesus' anguished cry from the cross, sin, guilt, forgiveness, redemption—all of these primordial religious experiences and master themes of Christianity are the raw materials of the vets' spiritual journey. If the Church is to understand and interpret the vets' experience, it, too, must grapple with God at the same primordial depth.

Tragically, the Church has played as yet almost no role in assisting the vets to readjust back in the world. The religious and moral dimensions of their crisis have passed unnoticed by religious leaders, theologians, and the people in the pews. But I still believe the Church has ahead of it two major tasks with regard to Vietnam vets. The first is the easier of the two. The Church must help the vets deal with their "dark night of the soul." The second task is far more difficult and even distasteful: the Church must open itself to hear the voices of Vietnam vets as an utterance of prophecy (in the authentic biblical sense), calling it to leave aside its unholy alliance with American religious mythology.

With respect to the first task, religious conservatives and liberals—if those terms retain any meaning—have been about equally inhospitable to the vets. Conservatives have spawned an ugly bastard child in Christian fundamentalism. This latter group—its adherents must be counted in the millions—continues to embody and articulate those features of American civil religion that vets in the field appropriately termed "chaplain bullshit." If anything, the situation is worse now than it was a few years ago. What the vets considered bullshit fifteen years ago hasn't changed.

Religious liberals fare little better. Smug and self-righteous, many of these well-intentioned people continue to represent the worst features of the antiwar movement of the sixties, with their inability to separate "the war from the warrior." They have caused much pain.

John Fergueson, a Marine Corps veteran of Vietnam who later became an Episcopal priest, recalls overhearing two fellow priests talking about him shortly after he was ordained. One remarked to the other, "There goes the baby killer who thinks he's a priest." Several years later Fergueson attended a conference on the spiritual life of the clergy. During a part of the presentation, the participants were invited to speak out loud about anything they were experiencing during prayer. He writes:

> Men would speak out and receive reassuring words and often a hug or touch of support.
> In this deepened experience of prayer, I was focused upon Viet Nam. Suddenly a wave of love and peace swept over me. I was overcome and blurted out, "Thank you for forgiving me about Viet Nam." There was silence. No reassuring words, no touches, no hugs. Just silence and the sound of one or two people leaving the room. I had just uttered the ultimate obscenity. I had put God—forgiveness—and Viet Nam together.[73]

Another Marine Corps vet, Timothy C. Sims, who served two tours in Vietnam and is a survivor of Khe Sanh, is now a Lutheran pastor and active-duty Navy chaplain. He writes:

Alexander Solzhenitsyn taught us what a gulag is. Gulags are Russian forced labor camps. But there are other kinds of gulags besides the state-run institutions. Gulags can also be unspoken societal conspiracies to overlook, avoid, ignore. During college, I entered the gulags of the ignored Vietnam vet.[74]

The "children of light" who proclaimed the war in Vietnam to be a moral outrage were certainly correct, but in relegating the vets to the role of "children of darkness," they demonstrated their own blindness and hypocrisy. Worse than their ignorance of the vets' real situation and their denial of society's role in the war is their refusal to extend the mercy of Christ to those whom they consider to be sinners. If Christian fundamentalism offers to vets the same idols that were shattered in Vietnam, Christian liberalism exhibits a spiritual pride that is also incompatible with the Gospel. These attitudes continue to keep vets away from the Church.

Where is the vet to go with his experience of God's absence from a world of evil? He cannot find a place among the religious fundamentalists who retreat from evil, denying its presence in their own souls by projecting it outward onto the Communists or the "secular humanists." For these people, the "evil empire" is always somewhere external to themselves and their own group. The vets know better, for Vietnam proved that evil resides within the hearts of all of us. Vets also know that authentic religion cannot be identified with American culture, with the endless pursuit of personal fulfillment, or even with feeling good about Jesus. The network of religious and emotional props that conservatives and fundamentalists construct to insulate themselves from evil are useless after Vietnam.

On the other hand, many religious liberals seem to believe that a sense of personhood and human fulfillment are the end products of religion. They believe that social activism must necessarily bring about a better society in this world. They try to fashion God's presence in the world according to their own tastes. While their efforts in behalf of peace and justice are noble indeed, they seem to overestimate their own power and consistently underestimate the power of evil. They seem to have little understanding of Job's question, and they possess no real "theology of the Cross."

Of course, there are millions of American Christians: Evangelical Protestants, mainline Protestants, Episcopalians, and Roman Catholics who fall into neither of these extremes. Unfortunately, the public perception of Christianity exaggerates the importance of these two positions. This creates the impression that these polarities somehow represent and express what the Church is about in this country. Nothing could be farther from the truth.

IN AND OUT OF DESPAIR

The wandering of Vietnam vets in and out of despair, the shattering of their faith, and their immersion in darkness are religious experiences of the first magnitude. In the midst of God's absence remains only his strange and haunting presence. Because of their own experience, vets can relate to the Church only in terms of its authentic religious experience.

Timothy Sims, like so many vets, "tried to exorcise God from my life, but his presence would not leave me alone." In what must have been terribly painful years in his spiritual journey, Sims came to understand that all he had was a "me and God experience." He now knows that "there are all kinds of Jesus-in-the-desert experiences, Jeremiah-in-despair experiences, and Paul-awaiting-trial experiences." Sims then connects the biblical experience with that of the vet in the "gulag."

"Wherever in the gulags of the world, there is a solitary man or woman who cries out in rage or fear or need, there is the 'me and God' experience."[75]

Returning to his own personal journey, Sims remembers that "me and God was not pleasant, it was agony, but it was all I had." God's love was maddening to him. "Never before had God been so really present as when, even in my rage, I could feel love near me, arms around me, tears washing me."[76]

Sims is now aware that he has had a mystical experience. He writes:

> My mystical experience of God's presence then is still more real than anything I have had since in the church. I suppose that is the gift of mystical encounter: the desert is a place of clear contrasts. Dark and light, cold and heat, hunger for the comfort of bread and hunger for deliverance from evil—these things tear away the accidents of time and place, and there is *apokalupsis* the "unveiling" of the mystery of God which God desires one to behold. My vision was of Heavenly Mother, crying and howling with me, seeking to hold me to her comforting breast; the vision was of heavenly Father, grieved and wounded with me, holding me with aching arms.
>
> God's mystic presence would not leave me alone so I decided to give his "dirty Bride" (the Church) another look.[77]

When Sims turned to the Church, he became a Lutheran, because a Lutheran chaplain had visited his unit near the end of the siege of Khe Sanh. Sims remembered him "preaching no sermon, simply going about among those of us who were left with bread saying, 'the body of Christ, the body of Christ'...with the smell of our dead buddies, stacked in empty bunkers, still in our noses, he walked among us with another broken body."[78]

Fergueson also makes the connection between the desert experience of the vets and the Church. He writes:

> We (Vietnam vets) are men and women "of sorrows and familiar with suffering." Thus, we are one with Jesus. We need to rise to new life. The church exists to proclaim this resurrection. In the Episcopal Church we state, "The mission of the church is to restore all persons to unity with God and each other in Christ."
>
> We, your brothers and sisters, children of God, who wear that yellow service ribbon with three red stripes are waiting to discover if that mission applies to us, or whether you will continue to make us the pariahs who silently bear what you are unwilling to face.[79]

Sims and Fergueson are not unique in the religious dimensions of their experience. The difference between them and thousands of other vets is only in their ability to use the language of Scripture and of the Christian mystics to understand and interpret the Vietnam experience. Both turn to the Church—even though it is indeed a "dirty Bride"—because the Church alone is called to reconcile all people to each other and all to God in Christ. There is simply nowhere else to go.

The mission of the Church to Vietnam vets—the first and easier of its two tasks—becomes clear when the true nature of the Vietnam experience is understood. If the anger at God and loss of faith, the dark night of the soul, is one stage of an authentic "me and God" relationship, then the Church must first of all provide some spiritual direction. The Church must reach into the reservoir of its own experience with God and with community, making its spiritual treasure truly accessible to angry, alienated veterans. It must try to incorporate the vets into its own life and worship.

Of course, the Church should assume an advocacy role on behalf of Vietnam vets in the same way it has for other groups on the fringes of society. The Church should also state very clearly that the responsibility for the Vietnam War—and for all wars—rests with the entire society. Most importantly, however, the Church must recognize, as Fergueson does, that "although most veterans resist the idea, they need to feel absolved... We need to feel reconciled to God, ourselves, our fellow citizens, and our former enemies."[80] This means that veterans must, above all else, be enabled to experience the healing, reconciling, and redemptive function of the Church.

There are a number of ways for the Church to reach out to vets. St. John's Episcopal Church in Los Angeles, which has already been mentioned in this book, furnishes one model. This parish provided both moral support and space for the Center for Veterans Rights during the years when Vietnam veterans were largely ignored. The rector of the church was on the center's board of directors and became personally involved in veteran's issues. I believe it is still necessary for some churches to provide this kind of support and involvement, but I think something more is now required of all churches. The ministry of healing and reconciliation that lies at the heart of the Gospel must be extended unambiguously and forcefully to veterans. In order to do this effectively, the Church must make it very clear that it is prepared to deal with every facet of human experience, including the horrible evils of modern war.

The Church must first open its arms to vets and make them feel completely at home in the community of faith, extending to them genuine love and warmth. Then it must communicate its willingness to listen to the "Vietnam question," which is their major spiritual burden. Once it has done these things, the Church must then provide competent spiritual directors for those who wander in the darkest night of the soul. A spiritual director in the classic sense is one who is both learned in biblical theology and deeply immersed in a life of prayer. Such a person has a profound grasp of his/her own dark side and yet has a deep and abiding sense of God's presence and of His endless mercy. A competent spiritual director knows both from personal experience and from a grasp of the biblical story what it means to wander in a spiritual desert and to find God in the most unlikely corners of the wasteland. Above all, the spiritual director must be open to the Spirit both in his/her own life and in the lives of those who seek counsel. The term "spiritual director" has fallen into some disfavor in our democratic and egalitarian culture, with new terms such as "soul friend" or "spiritual friend" displacing it. The name is not important, but the function is. Without a good deal of spiritual direction on the part of the Church, it will be almost impossible for most vets to enter more deeply into the mystic encounter with God begun in the religious wilderness of Vietnam.

Finally, the Church must find ways to include the Vietnam experience, with all its anger, guilt, and doubts, somewhere within the structure of corporate worship. Worship is the central act of the Christian community. In its public community prayer, the Church both opens itself to God and binds its members together. In the Christian context there is no knowledge of God except through communion with people, and in prayer we communicate not only with God but with each other at the deepest possible level of our beings. There is a solidarity in prayer, an inner center, a point beneath words and actions, where we meet as children in the presence of our Father. So our prayer begins *"Our Father"* for all prayer is social prayer.[81]

In prayer we know God in faith and love rather than through intellect. Prayer to some extent always entails an awareness of God as in a "cloud of unknowing." This is the reason prayer at a deep level is so important for Vietnam vets. Their experience of God is already shrouded in the type of darkness that characterizes the prayer of mystics in its beginning stages, but most of them have not yet begun to experience the blinding light of God's presence that marks the final stages of mystical prayer. I believe the haunting sense of a God who has been "flipped *off*" long before but who "will not leave me alone" is an invitation from God to the vet to enter into the kind of relationship with Him that is found in Scripture and has been described by centuries of saints and mystics.

Of course, the relationship is primarily between God and the individual vet, but the Church has the obligation to furnish spiritual direction, and more importantly, to include the vet within its own common life of worship. I offer one suggestion as to how the Church might initiate this process. Though there are differences among the various branches of the Church with respect to styles and emphases in public worship, these are no longer as great as we once believed. My own approach is, of course, the result of my participation in the prayer life of the Episcopal church with a long "incubation period" spent in Roman Catholic religious order (the Augustinians). What I have to say is heavily influenced by a very "catholic" understanding of the Eucharist, which will be familiar to Roman Catholics, Episcopalians, Eastern Orthodox, and Lutherans but is now becoming increasingly important to many others, as well.

The central act of worship in the Church is called by various names: the Eucharist, mass, the breaking of the bread, the Lord's Supper, divine liturgy. The Eucharist also sums up all of our life before God and provides us with a means of grace to live out our faith in the world. It is a source and center of our spiritual lives. Kenneth Leech, a Church of England priest, succinctly states our belief:

> So bread and wine, and also human persons, are transformed and in this action the Eucharist sums up and expresses the whole of Christian life and prayer. For in all life, the sanctifying power of the Spirit is funda-

mental. Unless the Spirit falls in flame, there is no life. All prayer, like all Eucharistic celebrations is, in the words of the Roman Missal, a "prayer of thanksgiving and sanctification."

The Eucharistic Prayer is the centre of all Christian prayer, the centre of all liturgy, the centre of our common life together, and is therefore extremely important that this Great Prayer, as it is sometimes called, should express as fully and completely as possible the beliefs and intentions of the church in this central act of its life.... The Eucharist is Christ, present and active now in the fullness of his redeeming work.[82]

Many vets feel themselves cut off from the worship of the Church because of Vietnam. Somehow they feel that Vietnam excludes them from the redeeming grace of God; hence, they are no longer at home in the worship of the Church, which so fully expresses its relationship to God in Christ. They have quite literally "excommunicated" themselves in the sense of breaking off all communion both with Christ in the Eucharist and with the Church. Reentry into public worship is a crucial step, but reentry must somehow include the Vietnam experience. I believe there is a way to do this.

Early in 1985 I participated with Walter Capps—who is a Lutheran—in a program for Vietnam veterans and other members of the surrounding community at a Roman Catholic retreat center in Santa Barbara, California. The theme of the day was "Ten Years After Vietnam: A Time for Healing." The day concluded with a "liturgy of reconciliation." This was simply a Eucharistic worship service that I composed based on the Episcopal Church's Book of *Common Prayer.* The three Scripture readings used were relevant to the issues of war and peacemaking. The prayers, including the prayer of consecration, were written around this theme. We confessed our sins, especially those of "violence and hatred," receiving for these sins the forgiveness of God as symbolized by the absolution of the priest. Hymns were selected according to the theme. The unity and deep yearning for the peace of mind that only reconciliation can achieve was more than evident at the service, and we each left deeply moved.

The next day I was in Las Vegas, Nevada, speaking to a regional training session of Vet Center counselors from the western United States. I mentioned the liturgy of the previous day in one of my talks. Afterward, a vet, a former Catholic, approached me and said, "Some of us feel there's no forgiveness for Vietnam." I replied, "You know better than that." He asked me to repeat the service of the previous day for himself and whomever he could find during the next few minutes before the noon break. We did—in a hotel room. Again, it was a very powerful and moving experience. Some of the vets present were Catholics from the state of New Mexico. I encouraged them to take a copy of the liturgy to Archbishop Robert F. Sanchez of Sante Fe and ask him to do something like it on a large and public scale.

On July 4, 1985, a special mass for Vietnam vets was celebrated at the Cathedral in Sante Fe and in five other Roman Catholic churches in New Mexico. The theme was the same—reconciliation, forgiveness, and the redeeming presence of God in Christ. Large numbers of vets attended. Some of those who were there called me to tell me how much it meant to them. Archbishop Sanchez wrote to tell me that he had forwarded information about the event to the National Liturgical Office in Washington "for their own review and, perhaps, follow-up. In any event, be assured that we will continue to work with our Vietnam veterans." I believe this is a marvelous beginning, but only a beginning. A copy of one of these liturgies is included in the appendix of this book in the hope that it will be modified, improved, and used widely.

THE PROPHETIC VOICE
AND AUTHENTIC RELIGION

The more difficult of the two tasks facing the Church with respect to the vets is that of allowing them to be a prophetic voice within American culture. I have already said that I believe Vietnam vets exercise a prophetic voice with respect to American society and its love affair with war.

Prophecy is not just a call to return to a moral way of life. It is a profoundly religious function. A prophet is one who speaks before others, communicating some aspect of divine revelation. To some it may seem ludicrous to make any connection between biblical prophecy and a ragtag bunch of vets, many of whom have lost their religious faith. I think a closer look is required.

The vets' painful encounter with God coincided with an unmasking of American religious mythology—a form of idolatry. The Church has been complicit in perpetrating—or at least tolerating—this mythology in America for more than three centuries. By opening its arms to Vietnam vets and incorporating their experience as its own, the Church becomes more aware of its complicity in the sins of idolatry and war. With this new awareness of its own past sins and failures, the American Church can then translate the vets' message into an authentic prophetic utterance about war.

For the vets, the discovery of the truth about war was connected with a bleak and painful dark night of the spirit. Greater exposure to the spiritual sufferings of the vets should bring about within the Church a recognition that the dark night of the soul is an authentic Christian mystical experience. The American Church has evaded the dark night through near-total immersion in a culture that seeks personal and national well-being at the expense of every other value. War has always served as a means to bring about personal glory and national hegemony, both of which "feel good" in our culture. In the life of Jesus, there is certainly a connection between His own suffering and His unwillingness to use violent means against those who persecuted Him. Vietnam vets confront the Church with its own superficial commitment to a Lord who endured His own terrible night of the spirit and commanded us to "take up your cross and follow me." Vets also remind the Church of Jesus' words and deeds connected with forgiveness of enemies and becoming peacemakers.

A prophet must always speak from within the authentic religious tradition. In fact, prophecy speaks first to the religious community and only then to the surrounding culture. If the Church takes the vets seriously, it must necessarily withdraw its support of American civil religion with its cult and glorification of war. This would, of course, have a tremendous impact on the entire culture. Decisions regarding the use of military force would have to be made without reference to a "city on the hill" theology. If Americans who are serious Christians were again called upon to go to war, they would have to struggle with the questions about war and the Gospel that the fourth-century Church confronted and that gave rise to the just-war doctrine. They would have to struggle mightily with the moral and religious questions involved in such a decision rather than merely taking mindless refuge in an idolatrous mythology.

In a church that took the vets seriously, any future American president who addressed a roomful of Evangelical preachers and stated his belief that another nation was the biblical embodiment of evil would be greeted by icy silence rather than by enthusiastic applause. A president who invoked Luke's Gospel in support of his defense budget would encounter ridicule rather than support. Clearly, the voice of the vets spoken within the Church and to the culture is prophetic, and much needed.

The prophetic voice of Vietnam vets begins as a call for

renewal within the Church not only in light of the vets' painful but authentic religious experience but in terms of the Gospel, as well. I offer these New Testament passages as an invitation to prayerful reflection.

You have heard the commandment, "An eye for an eye, a tooth for a tooth." But what I say to you is: offer no resistance to injury. When a person strikes you on the right cheek, turn and offer him the other. *(Matt. 5:38-39).*

You have heard the commandment, "You shall love your countryman but hate your enemy." My command to you is: love your enemies, pray for your persecutors. This will prove that you are sons of your heavenly Father, for his sun rises on the bad and the good, he rains on the just and the unjust. If you love those who love you, what merit is there in that? Do not tax collectors do as much? And if you greet brothers only, what is so praiseworthy about that? Do not pagans do as much? In a word, you must be made perfect as your heavenly Father is perfect. (Matt. *5:43-48)*

When His followers tried to defend Him with their swords in the garden on the evening of His arrest, Jesus told them: "Put back your sword where it belongs. Those who use the sword are sooner or later destroyed by it." (Matt. 26:52)

In His last moments of life, Jesus asked only one thing from His Father for those who had insulted, defeated, and murdered Him: forgiveness. "Father, forgive them; they do not know what they are doing." (Luke 23:34)

St. Paul, a former enemy of Jesus, himself no stranger to violence—nor to the night of the soul—wrote this about his Lord and the Church:

All this has been done by God, who has reconciled us to himself through Christ and has given us the ministry of reconciliation. I mean that God, in Christ, was reconciling the world to himself, not counting men's transgressions against them, and that he has entrusted the message of reconciliation to us. This makes us ambassadors for Christ, God as it were appealing through us. We implore you, in Christ's name: be reconciled to God! (2 Cor. 5:18-20)

VETS: DEEP SWIMMERS IN SHALLOW WATERS

Though the issues of war and peace are always the central focus of the Vietnam religious experience, other areas of American Christianity come under scrutiny as a result of taking the vets seriously. One of these is the American love affair with "therapy," which has had a significant impact on the Church.

Americans are engaged in a "nervous search for the true self." We have become a nation of autonomous, radically individualized selves seeking our own personal fulfillment with very little regard for other individuals except as they have impact on us. At least this seems to be the conclusion of Robert Bellab and four coauthors of a rather remarkable recent study of American life *Habits of the Heart.* The therapeutic self is "defined by its own wants and satisfactions, coordinated by cost-benefit calculation. Its social virtues are largely limited to empathic communication, truth-telling and equitable negotiation."[83] Largely a matter of style, there is very little substance to the therapeutic relationship. We are enabled to communicate better, but what do we communicate? It seems as if beneath it all "there is no there there."

As we have seen, the vets' experience points to the failure

of therapy to provide anything more than a useful tool for improving communication perhaps and for overcoming certain kinds of emotional stress. As valuable as it is, therapy cannot even begin to deal with the real underlying issues of Vietnam because it assigns no moral or religious significance to human activity. If they have performed no other service to their society, Vietnam vets have demonstrated that war, a major human activity, cannot be considered apart from morality and religion. If this is the case, can the rest of life be that different? The incessant search for a perfectly fulfilled self is nothing more than undisguised narcissism. The Church has only begun to address this issue—its contact with the vets should provide further stimulus to confront the phoniness and inner emptiness engendered by the therapeutic mind-set.

The Vietnam vet story runs cross grain to these prevailing currents in American culture. Vets themselves have had to move beyond therapy. They have been forced to confront issues far beyond their own narrow interests. Years spent in isolation brought them to a new and deeper understanding of community. Most important, they struggled with God in a strange and hostile environment and found that God would not let them go.

Indeed the vets may dare to speak with some authority to the Church, for American religion is characterized by a withdrawal into a purely private spirituality that isolates the self from other people, from concern for peace and justice issues, and from public life. For many people, the Church has become just another of the institutions through which a person may find fulfillment. The authors of *Habits of the Heart* report a tendency among evangelical churches to "thin the biblical language of sin and redemption to an idea of Jesus as the friend who helps us find happiness and self-fulfillment." At the same time, the Roman Catholic church, which seems more resistant to cultural tides, is also deeply affected by the therapeutic mind-set. A recent national sample of Catholics, when asked what direction their church should take in the future, asked for "personal and accessible priests" and "warmer, more personal parishes." Among the thousands of local churches in the United States, with an enormous range of variation in doctrine, discipline, and worship, most define themselves as "communities of personal support."[84]

Church communities should, of course, be warm and supporting, but they must be far more, for the Christian faith is first of all an encounter with the risen Christ who Himself assembles the community, giving it a mission and purpose for all time. Vietnam provides contemporary evidence that sin, emptiness, and the gulags of the world are also part of human experience. More than any other Americans, the vets can testify that the Church is called to be a servant to all humanity not merely by embracing its various struggles to overcome oppression but by extending to a very broken and empty world its own experience of a gracious and living God.

CHAPTER SEVEN:
WHAT IT ALL MEANS

The psalmist surely speaks for the vets when he cries out, "My soul is full of troubles and my life draws near to Scheol... Thou has put me in the depths of the pit, in the regions dark and deep." (Ps. 88:3 and 6) But Vietnam is not the only experience that plunges us into the lowest pit. The psalmist spoke to a universal human condition as he lamented and cried out to God from the depths of misery. It is a rare person indeed who is not moved by the raw power of the Psalms.

Many people feel the approach of spiritual desolation in their lives—the condition that afflicted the psalmist—but they fend it off, seeking again the "warm fuzzies" they have come to identify with religious faith. "Happy face" religion and "have a nice day" spirituality are pervasive. Because they cling to these religious toys, many people are forced to deny their true feelings, and they remain spiritual adolescents all their lives.

The Vietnam veterans' spiritual experience has much to say to all those whose lives are more desperate than they care to admit. Having confronted God in the desert of their souls, the vets provide a contemporary model for the anguish of Job, the cry of the Psalmist, and even of the agony of Jesus himself. Not much is said these days in American Christianity about this dimension of religious experience. It seems that all must be sweetness and light. Martin Marty calls the dark night of the soul "the winter of the heart." Disturbed by the fact that those who bask in the summer of the spirit seem to have preempted American religious life, Marty writes:

> Who tends the spirit where winter takes over?... In our generations...to mention spirituality is to evoke images only of the long-day suns of summers. Those who begin with a sense of the void, the Absence, who live with dullness of soul, feel left out when others speak only of such bright spirituality.
>
> Picture someone hungry for a warming of the spirit. He calls a friend who is advertised as spirit-filled. "Praise the Lord!" she responds, as she picks up the telephone. The two meet in person. One is chilly but open to stirrings, the other well characterized as full of stir. What transfer of spirit can occur when the filled person is compulsive about the summer and sunshine in her heart? Never does a frown cloud her face. Lips, once drawn tight in disapproval, are now drawn tight in a cosmetic smile. "The Lord wills it." Never does the storm of a troubled heart receive its chance to be heard. The Lord has satisfied every need, one hears, so it would be a sin to stare once more at the void within. Christ is the answer, the spirit is warm and no chill is ever allowed between the boards or around the windows of the soul.[85]

The winter of the spirit comes about for many reasons, the most common being spiritual growth. A person who advances in serious prayer always experiences what the mystics call the "dark night of the senses," a period in which the emotional and cultural "props" simply give way. No longer does it "feel good" to pray, go to church, or live a virtuous life. Perseverance in prayer leads into an even bleaker "dark night of the soul," characterized by doubts about God and despair of one's own capacity to continue in God's presence. For the mystics these conditions are but a necessary prelude to a "transforming union" with God. Before one is able to attain this kind of union with God, the soul is purified of attachments to sin and even of attachments to one's favorite religious feelings and images of the Divine. In this state of mystical union, one realizes that all religious images are inadequate and that no language or set of concepts can truly express the divine reality that has grasped the soul. The presence of God transcends any religious feelings, or lack of them. Though the mystic is undoubtedly a virtuous person by any human standards, he remains profoundly aware of sin, weakness, and nothingness before God because he now comprehends in a very real way who God is.

Winter of the spirit touches in some way all those who are serious about prayer. Its icy blasts also chill the hearts of those stricken with terminal illness and those who suffer the loss of a spouse or a child. If we live long enough and are honest with ourselves, all of us will know to some degree the winter of the soul. Though much of American religious life subverts this kind of experience, there are certainly many people with whom to share the burden of painful personal loss, people who will accompany us on the journey into bleakness. Guides in sufficient numbers are also available for those serious Christians who embark for the first time on the mystical journey. Though all those who feel the touch of darkness upon the spirit can learn from the vets' experience, I believe the Vietnam journey out of the night speaks especially to a particular situation—the onset of spiritual bleakness that occurs when one confronts in a serious way the profoundly troubling issues of peace and justice in the world.

All God's great servants whose stories are told in Scripture lived in a harsh and brutal world. They did not attempt to deceive themselves about their surroundings by pretending things were really okay, after all; rather, by coming to grips with human evil, they knew God in a mystical union that changed them completely. Countless other people throughout history and into our own times have also experienced God's transforming presence as the final outcome of a personal struggle with the power of evil in the world.

Paradoxically, though they accepted the harshness of the world around them, the prophets, apostles, saints, and mystics were acutely aware of God's command that justice be done, that the poor and oppressed be cared for. Their lives were consumed by a passion for justice, and they did as much as they could to bring about the biblical vision of peace and justice in a very unjust and warring world. The quest for a deep personal relationship with God was for these people inseparable from a struggle with the powers of darkness that are unleashed in the human community.

This paradigm provided by biblical figures and mystics is the only prism through which the Vietnam religious experience can be interpreted. Vietnam, in turn, is an opening into the very harsh world of the late twentieth century—a world against which we Americans try to construct barriers of myth and fantasy. When we inquire where God is in this kind of world and what we are doing to each other in it, and when we further inquire how we should respond to God and to each other, we are likely to become deeply troubled in spirit.

The religious night of Vietnam was brought on by war, the most devastating and tragic of human activities. Through Vietnam the brutality of the modern world was thrust upon our national consciousness. Prolonged isolation of the vets was society's signal that such a world was too disconcerting to consider. Only now, at some distance from the war and during a period of national nostalgia for the good old days when wars were glorious and America stood tall, has the public been able to accept the vets. As we romanticize the past, we also continue headlong in our search for the quick fix to economic and political ills, and above all, we reaffirm our commitment that life must be always therapeutic and self-fulfilling. Psychic and spiritual defenses continue to keep the truth about the world from reaching our consciousness. That life is brutish, short, and most unfilling for billions of our fellow humans is no concern of ours—or so we try to convince ourselves. The question we must ask ourselves is how this condition of the world enters into our own personal search for God.

A great many Americans make little connection between themselves and the rest of humanity in their quest for God. Much of the religious renewal now sweeping the country is in reality nothing more than a defense mechanism that allows us to fulfill our personal spiritual needs—the criterion of fulfillment being how we feel about our relationship with God—without so much as a passing glance at the state of humanity. We concentrate religiously on ourselves and how we feel. We speak in tongues, meet in prayer groups, become very supportive of each other in cozy settings, and become quite comfortable about the work of the Spirit in our lives.

These renewal movements have indeed been of great benefit to the Church and to the individuals who participate in them. I respect these people for undertaking a genuine search for God in their lives, but I am continually amazed at how little real understanding they have of the suffering world in which they live. They are "Spirit filled" and most enthusiastic about their own relationship with God, but the question of how God relates to the rest of the world seems unimportant.

On the other hand, social activists, those who devote much of their time and energy to causes for the betterment of humanity, often convey the impression of giving little real thought to God. Every issue is conceived solely in political and economic terms. A great many activists do, in fact, operate only on the political and not the religious level of concern. Social activists who have no deeper spiritual roots often "burn out" after a brief and perfunctory fling at being "concerned." Look at today's yuppies who were yesterday's flower children.

Of course, there are still the uncounted and largely unnoticed people who combine a concern for personal spirituality with a passion for peace and justice. Clustered in small groups, usually around some local parish church, these people still try to follow the Gospel mandate with respect to becoming peacemakers and feeding the hungry, but they receive very little public notice.

The dichotomy between religion on the one hand and a concern for the world on the other is a serious problem in modern times. Several significant streams of nineteenth- and twentieth-century thought either exclude God from consideration or deny His existence because of a supposed opposition between the good of humanity and the search for God. Marxism, European existentialism, and the American philosophy of pragmatism have been influential systems of thought in our time, and all pose in one way or another the opposition between God and humanity. It seems that the American Church has accepted this dichotomy, certainly not in principle but in the way many of its members seem forced to choose between a serious personal search for God or a commitment to peace and justice in the world. The dichotomy is both unbiblical and tragic.

The faith of Vietnam veterans was shattered on the rocks of war. The "altered consciousness" of the world that Peter Marin notes among vets is an altered religious consciousness, a changed awareness of who God really is. The journey out of spiritual desolation for a vet—or for anyone similarly touched by the great evils of humanity—must include some resolution of the problem of "God and the others," and not only the "God and me" question. It may be that Christian faith ultimately means that I "accept Jesus as my personal Savior," but "personal Savior" is too small a notion. Either Jesus is Lord of all the world, or He has no real significance.

Vietnam vets are by no means the only people who have experienced this dislocation of religious consciousness that plunges them into the dark night of the soul. During the years I worked in Los Angeles, I encountered quite a few very committed and deeply religious people working in public agencies, poverty centers, church projects, and various other efforts to alleviate the relentless problems of poverty and unemployment in that city. Most of them were lay people, but some were pastors of churches, priests and ministers, and some were Catholic nuns. As I got to know these marvelous people, many would confide their own state of soul. They would often describe a condition not unlike that of the vets with whom I was working. The doubts and questions would surface: "Where is God in all this?" Touched by evil on a much larger scale than that of mere personal suffering, these true servants of the Lord experienced a deep anguish, sometimes bordering on despair. I will always remember a phone call from a very saintly woman, a Catholic sister, who had spent years in Central America and who was then working at a church center in the midst of one of L.A.'s worst ghettos. Her task was to find shelter, food, and clothing for people who had been refused assistance by the county welfare agency; she lived with human misery every day. When I picked up the phone, she identified herself and said, "Bill, I can't stand it anymore. It's just too overwhelming." We talked for a while, and she concluded that she would indeed stay on but that she would have to deepen her own prayer life if she was to survive spiritually in her situation. I wondered at the time how it was possible for her to come any closer to God than she already was. Whatever she did in her own personal spiritual life, she was still on the job when I left Los Angeles. For her and for others like her, the quest for God included a willingness to endure the night of the spirit one always faces when confronted by monstrous evil.

Serious encounters with evils like hunger, poverty, homelessness, and war almost always result in a sense of personal powerlessness, emptiness, and spiritual darkness. Thomas Merton is correct: The metaphysical concept of emptiness is convertible in economic terms into poverty, being poor, having nothing." Anyone who lives in poverty or deprivation, anyone who encounters war, and anyone who takes these realities seriously is never again the same. The dark night of the soul becomes a part of one's own spirituality. Many people instinctively know this and so draw back from involvement with these issues even though they are aware of the Gospel mandate to become peacemakers, feed the hungry, visit those in prison. I believe this is the reason for the widespread reluctance among American Christians to incorporate these concerns into their own spiritual lives. They sense that the nice warm feeling they have about God will leave them, only to be replaced by desolation of spirit. Like Vietnam vets, they might be confronted by Job's question, or even worse, by Christ on the cross.

COMING TO GRIPS WITH GOD

Vietnam vets and others who have felt the desolation of humanity's gulags have ample resources to negotiate their journey out of the night. Scripture, the writings of the mystics, and guidance from those with personal experience of winter in the spirit are sufficient maps for the journey as long as one remembers that God alone is the light at the end of the tunnel.

"ME AND GOD"

Whenever one cries out in rage against God, as did the ex-Marine we met in the first chapter, or when one spends years "flipping off" God, as have so many vets, there is a "me and

God" experience that is not entirely unlike that of the psalmist or Job. If one wishes to continue the relationship with God begun in this experience, it is important to be still and silent for a time. Another image is helpful at this point: that of the "cloud." This kind of religious experience resembles traveling through a thick and impenetrable fog or low cloud. Anyone who drives in this kind of weather must first of all recognize the weather conditions and then slow down and sometimes even stop. The same is true in the spiritual journey. The famous but anonymous author of a very significant fourteenth-century work of mysticism first describes the condition and then offers some advice.

> You see nothing and feel nothing but a kind of darkness about your mind, as it were, a cloud of unknowing.
> You will feel nothing and know nothing except a naked intent toward God in the depths of your being. Try as you might, this darkness and this cloud will remain between you and your God. You will feel frustrated for your mind will be unable to grasp him and your heart will not relish the delight of his love. But learn to be at home in this darkness. Return to it as often as you can, letting your spirit cry out to him whom you love. For if, in this life, you hope to see and feel God as he is in himself it must be within this darkness and this cloud...God in his goodness will bring you to a deeper experience of himself.[86]

The anonymous author's advice that we should learn to be at home in the darkness and even return to it as often as we can seems at first glance to be madness, yet this is the essential first step in the journey out of the night. Earlier in the book I stated that all religious language is necessarily symbolic—and even that is inadequate, because no mental images or language patterns can convey adequately the reality of God. Human knowledge with respect to God always functions within a cloud of unknowing simply because God is God and we are creatures with finite minds. This does not mean that one cannot learn about God from study of the Bible and from theological reflection but that the object of study, reflection, and prayer is a Person who is essentially beyond the reach of the human mind: He who told Moses, "No one can see my face and live."

The fourteenth-century work is a guidebook for those who wish to practice contemplative prayer. This form of prayer is essentially simple and uncomplicated, but to reach it, one must first strip away all illusions about oneself, others, and God. To acknowledge the darkness and even to return to it voluntarily is only to acknowledge the truth about God and about oneself. This is extraordinarily painful, because the primordial human temptation is "to be like the gods who know what is good and what is bad." (Gen. 3:5) When we are enveloped by the cloud, we are aware of the distance between God and ourselves. The cloud is frustrating at first, but by learning to live in it and returning to it, one gradually learns to grasp God in the only way He can really be known.

Vets and others whose neat notions of God, self, and the world have been shattered by evil of great magnitude have been thrust unwillingly into the same condition of spiritual darkness that mystics know is the prerequisite for the deepest knowledge of God possible in this life. The first voluntary step in the journey out of night is to cease the frantic efforts to escape from the darkness, realizing that one already has begun to grasp God in a very different way—this is true even though one wants nothing further to do with God. The painful and haunting presence of God, even among vets who have attempted for years to dismiss him, is a fair indication of God's tenacity. The poet Francis Thompson likened God to a hound who pursues a person "down the nights and down the days." Escape and evasion tactics—at which many vets are expert—do not work against God. One must first stop running in the darkness and allow the "hound of heaven" to catch his quarry.

In practical terms this means, first of all, that the "God question" must be pursued openly rather than left to simmer on the back burner of the mind. For those who wish to face the issue in the context of Christian faith, the focus—even though it be in anger—must be directly on God. One must become aware that this is truly a "me and God" relationship, however uncomfortable it may be. In order to create the space for this awareness to grow, one must attain some degree of inner solitude—a condition easier to achieve in a spiritual desert than in the noisy atmosphere of "juice and joy" religion.

The awareness of God that bubbles to the surface in these moments of desert solitude may be quite different from anything one has experienced in the past. It may, in fact, seem quite alien and even irreligious. Contemporary American Christianity leaves little room for this kind of experience. The prevailing religious current seems to require "the convention of speaking of God, Jesus Christ, or the Holy Spirit primarily as though they were persons who are somehow to be intimately known as lover, companion, friend or parent."[87] This sense of an intimate, tender presence of God is exactly what one loses in a combat zone or in the other wastelands of the world. The religious condition that frequently supplants it is

> an intense intuition of there being something elusive, haunting, indirect, yet utterly compelling about which life relentlessly revolves. There is a sense of being drawn or pursued by something that is never quite tangible, that never quite allows any sense of a face-to-face meeting.[88]

Though this type of religious experience runs counter to what a person may have known during an earlier and more innocent period of life, it is quite biblical. The God revealed in the Hebrew Scripture is intensely personal but always obscure, and He is frequently encountered in a desert or on a lonely mountaintop. In the New Testament, Jesus is recognized as Lord in His resurrection from the dead, but the risen Lord always goes on ahead of His disciples into Galilee and then ascends to the Father. He is with them, but at the same time He is absent and beyond them. The risen Lord is "less of a beloved presence than of a driving absence or the calling forth of a longing in the disciples"[89]

I believe the journey in spiritual darkness ultimately brings one to perceive God in this fashion. Perhaps a more intimate and tender sense of divine presence returns for a time—I know a number of combat veterans who have regained or acquired for the first time a powerful awareness of Jesus as friend—but most often the Lord seems to be saying, as he did to Mary Magdalene, "Do not touch me."

Vietnam, identified already as an ethical wilderness, must now become for the vets their own equivalent of the Bible's deserts, places of emptiness where one most often meets God. For others, like the Catholic sister in Los Angeles, who cry out in anguish from other wastelands, the desert is never far from them.

If one stops and listens in the bleakness of the gulag desert and in the darkest part of the spiritual night, one finds God as a mysterious presence at the horizon of life. The only way to come closer is to follow the elusive Person who both pursues and goes on ahead. Job, Moses, the psalmist, and the disciples of Jesus discovered this truth. This is why the anonymous author suggests that we learn to be at home in the cloud, returning to it as often as we can.

COMPLETING THE JOURNEY

The journey out of the night seems at first to be a uniquely personal pilgrimage in which other people play no significant role, but this is never the case. In the first place, our primary contact with God is through love. "No one can comprehend the uncreated God with his knowledge; but each one, in a different way, can grasp him fully through love."[90] Love of God is inseparable from love of neighbor; in fact,

> If anyone says, "my love is fixed on God," yet hates his brother, he is a liar. One who has no love for the brother he has seen cannot love the God he has not seen. The commandment we have from him is this: whoever loves God must also love his brother. (1 John 4:20-21)

Questions such as "Where was God in Vietnam?" or "Why does God permit worldwide poverty and hunger?" will always baffle the intellect, because God's purposes can never be fully understood. I am sure one of the great joys of eternal life will be the knowledge of how all the loose ends of human history finally weave together. Paul must have felt this way when he wrote, "Now we see indistinctly, as in a mirror; then we shall see face to face. My knowledge is imperfect now; then I shall know even as I am known." (1 Cor. 13:12) But we should not deceive ourselves: God's absence from the gulags of the world is more than just an unanswerable question; it is primarily a matter of human choice. If we grasp God most clearly through love and if love for God, whom we cannot see, is impossible apart from love for our brothers and sisters, whom we can see, then it becomes clear why we cannot feel the presence of God in the midst of war and in other situations in which hatred abounds.

War is an explosion of hatred into systematic and ruthless violence. Its savagery is beyond description. War represents a complete breakdown in the virtue of love among those who share a common humanity under God. If we take seriously the passage from 1 John, we must admit that the love of God is incompatible with the kind of hatred war unleashes. Cut off from love, we are cut off from God in the only avenue of access our limited nature really possesses. Isolation from God under these conditions brings about a different kind of spiritual night than that which we have already discussed. The darkness that closes in upon us when our souls are pervaded with hatred is not the same as that which afflicted Job and the psalmist. Neither is this the kind of cloud the anonymous author counsels us to seek. As long as hatred persists, we cannot grasp God in any way. The journey out of night requires that we shed our hatred of fellow men and women. If we are unwilling to take this step, we condemn ourselves to flounder for the rest of our lives in a state of oppressive and even unbearable spiritual darkness.

The second step in the journey out of night for vets is to walk away from the anger, rage, and hatred that are the war's continuing residue. One cannot make a lifetime career out of hating the Vietnamese—or Lyndon Johnson, Richard Nixon, and Jane Fonda, either. A person must do more than merely "sort out" the issues left over from the war in a rap group or some other comfortable setting. Insight into the real nature of one's problems, the companionship of other vets, and feeling good about oneself again are necessary to the healing process, but much more is required. The violence of war produces a violence in the soul that endures in countless subtle forms.

In order to complete the journey out of spiritual night, a vet must do a real moral inventory, discovering who he still hates and what kind of violence still lurks within his soul. He must then decide to walk away from it—filter it out of his thinking and feelings. In this regard, the "healing of memories" is crucial. One must confront the memories that engender hate—in therapy if necessary—then let go of them. In a religious sense this means handing them over to God. If this means laying aside the "warrior myth," so be it. It may be that a vet was indeed "the best there was" in combat and that he "never lost a battle," but that's all in the past. Every vet knows that there are a thousand ways to keep alive the very seductive warrior myth about himself—"nobody hassles me." If one is to live out the myth throughout the rest of life, there must be frequent trips to the source of psychic energy that fuels the myth: hatred, rage, love of violence. Like the alcoholic who must admit that he is powerless over alcohol and then make minute-by-minute decisions not to drink, a vet must admit to being powerless in the face of hatred and violence and then make continual decisions not to imbibe.

Similarly, people who choose to become seriously involved in the issues of peace and justice that threaten to overwhelm our civilization usually begin to realize they are confronted by a subtle but almost transcendent evil. Hatred is deeply embedded, if not within their own souls, in the world's structures and institutions. Nuclear weapons, for example, are, as Michael Walker reminds us, "not encompassable within the familiar moral world." The mere existence of such instruments of destruction is inseparable from an intent to use them. They are, after all, on line, fully deployed, and programmed to reach their targets. This deployment/intent bespeaks a human capacity for monstrous evil. This is true despite the denial systems feeding into the belief that these weapons will never be used. When one begins to pierce the political rhetoric, mythology, and rationalizations surrounding nuclear weapons, one becomes aware of the incredible immorality at the heart of modern civilization. World hunger, genocide, domestic poverty and unemployment, ruthless and oppressive acts by governments around the globe—all are indications of the violence that springs from humanity's hatreds. The world's gulags create the night of the spirit because they provide overwhelming evidence of our brutality and lack of love for one another. Anyone who attempts to work in the gulags and struggle against these evils learns a depressing truth about humanity and runs the risk of entering a dark night of the spirit.

If the vets must walk away from inner violence, which continues to scar the soul long after the war is over, so, too, must those actively concerned for peace and justice withstand the temptation to respond in kind to the "principalities and powers," the presence of evil that soon becomes personally oppressive. There is no such thing as a shoot-out at high noon with the forces of violence. Once one assumes the weapons of this spiritual enemy, one has lost the battle. We must love those brothers and sisters whom we do see in this world, or else we may make no claim that we love the God who is unseen and beyond us, and yet so intimately present within.

This brings us to the penultimate step in the journey out of night. It is not enough to walk away from monstrous evil. Its power is too strong. It pursues us into the corners of our soul. Love is a positive virtue demanding its own kind of action. The third step requires action in the face of pervasive hatred and its multiple offspring. The raw material for action of this kind is abundant among Vietnam vets. In our discussion of vets "marching along together again," we explored their desire to turn America around and even to change the world. In reaching out to each other (so obvious in the Vet Centers), they have contacted others, and the circle continues to widen. Men who previously could not admit love into their lives have become loving husbands and fathers. Women who went to the limits of their capacities for healing as nurses in Vietnam continue on as healers in the larger community. The moral seriousness beyond therapy is another indication of an intent to overcome both violence in the soul and brutality in the world. The primary point of contact with others and with God, love, blossoms even in the hearts of those who retain some smoldering resentments.

The pain of the world, which Marin believes is the burden of Vietnam vets, is shared by many others who are not vets but whose spiritual lives have taken on some of the same kind of scars. Those who have made the connection between peace, justice, and their own spiritual lives—one now meets them in parish groups, working in soup kitchens, helping refugees, searching for ways to move beyond war—have already taken this long step out of the darkness that always surrounds evil. Having confronted the incredible immorality of injustice, they have not flinched but have entered the fray. These are people who, like Mason, have made the "last commitment worthy of a lifetime to fight for peace in each of our hearts against the fierce enemies of our darkest natures," men and women who have understood a profound spiritual truth.

It may seem no more than pious but irrelevant platitude to emphasize love in the face of humanity's most consuming hatreds; the word, after all, has been reduced in meaning to almost nothing in our sentimental culture. Its New Testament use, however, is quite different. Christian love has God for its principal object and expresses itself in obedience to His commandments. When exercised toward others, love is not an impulse from the feelings, nor does it always go according to one's natural inclinations. It does not only spend itself on those for whom a person has some deep feeling or affinity, but it seeks the welfare of all and does evil toward no one. Love *(agape)* in the New Testament is a very powerful word.

Clearly, this kind of love is the work of a lifetime. It goes beyond—though it does not exclude—romantic love or the love of friendship. It is an enduring virtue, a "habit of the heart," something that stays with a person in periods of spiritual darkness as well as in the good times of life. It is also a gift of God and our means of most immediate access to Him.

Love of this kind seems like an impossible ideal. A vet and fellow VA employee with whom I had many stimulating discussions was fond of telling me that the Christian notion of love is meaningless "because it doesn't work in the twentieth century." My reply was simply that it didn't work any better in the first century. Whether it works or not to achieve any specific set of goals is not the point. Love represents God's design for all humanity; it is an ideal that is supposed to shape the lives of individual Christians, determining their attitudes and behavior toward every person on the face of the earth. The Church and its attitude toward the world must be governed by love, as well. The point is not that we achieve love in its fullness at any given moment in life but rather that we always strive toward it in everything we do.

Apart from love on this scale, which both dispels hatred from the crevices of the soul and brings about a commitment to turn things around in an evil world, there is no journey out of spiritual darkness. The winter of the spirit is really an invitation to enter into the deeper warmth and light of God's presence.

The New Testament invitation to enter into this kind of relationship with God and with others is, of course, the Sermon on the Mount (Matt. 5-7). Perhaps the clearest and most specific expression of the desire to love in this way is found in the prayer of a thirteenth-century man who indeed came very close to living it to perfection: Francis of Assisi. During his lifetime Francis experienced the bleakest of spiritual deserts, the most transparent openness to God, and a pervasive and contagious joy. He was an activist and a mystic, a mover and shaker of his times who nevertheless remained passive and silent in the transforming presence of God. He sets the pace for all of us who have been touched by the deepest pain and sin of the world:

Lord, make us instruments of your peace.
  Where there is hatred, let us sow love.
  where there is injury, pardon;
  where there is discord, union;
  where there is doubt, faith;
  where there is despair, hope;
  where there is darkness, light;
  where there is sadness, joy.
Grant that we may not so much seek
  to be consoled as to console;
  to be understood as to understand;
  to be loved as to love.
For it is in giving that we receive;
  it is in pardoning that we are pardoned; and
  it is in dying that we are born to eternal life.

The final step in the journey out of the night is more diffi-cult than the others. The unknown author tells us that there are times when we are seeking God in the cloud of unknowing and feeling far from Him when we must do one more thing. The author tells us to "fashion a cloud of forgetting beneath you, between you and every created thing." He/she continues:

> Every time I say "all creatures," I refer not only to every created thing but also to all their circumstances and activities. I make no exception. You are to concern yourself with no creature whether material or spiritual nor with their situation and doings whether good or ill. To put it briefly, during this work (prayer, the contem-plation of God's presence) you must abandon them all beneath the cloud of forgetting.
>
> For although at certain times and in certain circum-stances it is necessary and useful to dwell on the partic-ular situation and activity of people and things, during this work it is almost useless.[91]

When Job finally experienced God as the one who had "stretched out the measuring line" of the world, he was awestruck and speechless before God, his question no longer had any meaning. There was indeed a cloud of forgetting between Job and his world. At that moment he was in contact with God, and nothing else mattered. Moses before the burning bush and on Mount Sinai, Isaiah, Peter, James, and John on the mountain of the Transfiguration, the disciples of the risen Lord, Paul on the road to Damascus—all experienced a moment in which nothing else except God had any meaning for them. They all returned to their daily concerns, but they carried the experience with them throughout their lives.

What this means for Vietnam vets and others who have engaged in serious and even angry dialogue with God about the world's gulags is conceptually simple but quite difficult to implement. After having jettisoned the easy God of American mythology in favor of the One who can be known only in a cloud of unknowing and then having striven to banish hatred from the soul, living according to a deeper kin of love, a person may then become aware that a final act of faith is necessary. This act of faith requires that one place oneself, one's family, friends and enemies, the world and all its gulags in the hands of God.

The angry challenge hurled at God by vets and others who demand His presence in a malignant world is finally countered by a challenge from God. The challenge is simply to call Him "Father," as Jesus did. When we do this in terms of the prayer that Jesus taught us, we first concentrate on God exclusively: "Our Father, who are in heaven, hallowed be thy Name." At that moment everyone and everything that is not God are under a "cloud of forgetting." At that moment in our relationship with God we say of all else. "It don't mean nothin.'" This moment is essential, but it does not linger for long. Once we have focused on God in the Lord's Prayer, we immediately shift to present needs, for we are also demanding of God that His kingdom come, His will be done on earth as it is in heaven. We pray for daily bread and deliverance from evil. When we ask forgiveness for our own sins—our own participation in creating the world's gulags—we also ask God to make His forgiveness of us contingent upon our own forgiveness of our enemies. When one has demanded of God an accounting for His absence, God responds by an invitation to enter into the cloud to find the answer.

Paradoxically, this cloud of forgetting in no way diminishes one's human loves and commitments; it enhances them tremendously. Those engaged in "turning America" or the world, those discovering the joys of love in marriage and parenthood, and all who have found the type of love that opens the door to God again are invited to deepen these loves. Love in all the senses we have come to understand it remains and is immeasurable enriched by the love of God. But the point at which the darkness of soul begins to lift is that moment when God becomes such a powerful presence that a person is compelled to say of everyone and everything else, "It don't mean nothin.'"

The biblical model for this type of response to God in the midst of spiritual darkness is Jesus. Jesus had been the object of hatred and a victim of violence. He had been consumed in one of the world's gulags. As death approached, He cried out in terrible agony of spirit: "My God, my God, why have you forsaken me." (Matt. 27:46) The words are those of the psalmist (Ps. 22), and the anguish runs throughout the Psalm:

> O my God, I cry out by day,
>   and you answer not;
> by night and there is no
>   relief for me...
> But I am a worm, not a man;
>   the scorn of men, despised by people...
> I am like water poured out;
>   all my bones are wracked...

> They have pierced by hands
> and my feet;
> I can count all my bones.

That Jesus was overcome by the darkest of spiritual nights is not in question. Even when overcome by the power of the surrounding darkness, however, Jesus placed everything in the hands of the Father: "Father, into your hands I commend my spirit." (Luke: 46) His agony was unrelieved, and yet Jesus gave Himself—and the world—over into the hands of God. This example of Jesus in the most difficult of all transitions—from despair to trust in God—is the model; for *The Cloud of Unknowing*, for other Christian mystics, and for all Christians. I believe the act of trust in God made in the deepest agony of soul is the most difficult of all religious acts; it is also the most Christ-like.

It may be possible to spend a lifetime as a faithful Christian without ever entering into the realms of spirit we have been discussing. "Happy face" faith and love are authentic and may be sufficient if one never experiences the winter of the spirit. Vietnam veterans and others who have confronted the world's pervasive evil no longer have the luxury of swimming on the surface of religious life. Having been pulled into the depths, one must learn to swim underwater.

Ultimately, the passage from darkness to light is God's free gift and not ours to take. The promise of Scripture, however, is that He does indeed lead us from bondage into the promised land, from death to new life, from darkness into light. Once Jesus placed himself in the hands of the Father, He died. God's answer was then revealed in the raising of Jesus from the dead. Far from being a "pie in the sky" postponement of deliverance from evil to a future life, the resurrection is a present reality in the lives of believers. As the risen Lord encountered Saul on the road to Damascus, He encounters each of us on the paths of our own lives. Paul tells us that "just as Christ was raised from the dead by the glory of the Father, we too might live a new life." (Rom. 6:4) The "new life" is an overpowering awareness that in the risen Lord a new power is at work in the world—and in ourselves. This new power contains the seeds of destruction for the world's gulags—and the destruction of the sin within ourselves. Sin and death are still very much present, but they have been robbed of their ultimate power. Darkness remains, but now "a light shines on in darkness, a darkness that did not overcome it." (John 1:5). The steps suggested in this chapter for the journey out of the night are simply means to open ourselves to the risen Lord, who Himself brings us into the light.

Christian faith is never utopian. It does not place any hope in some evolutionary scheme by which humanity undergoes a mutation that filters out evil. Christian faith holds that God transforms our entire history not through some organic process but by His own unique creative power and in His own good time. In Christ, God revealed Himself as the One who has raised and will raise the dead, as the One who has shattered and will continue to shatter all human expectations. In Christ, God has begun to liberate humanity from sin, suffering, and death, and He will make the world new at the end of the ages. Passage out of the night consists in being gripped by the Spirit, who enables us to understand and to take part in this work of God.

The journey out of the night is the work of a lifetime. On the one hand, it requires complete passivity in the hands of God and an unconditional openness to His will; on the other, it requires of us unceasing activity as God's agents and instruments of peace and justice in a world of evil. In this regard, there is a certain irony in the question asked of God "Where were You in Vietnam?" The question comes full circle when one allows God to ask in return, "Where were you in Vietnam? When this kind of dialogue with God becomes possible, one is already under way in the journey out of the night.

CHAPTER EIGHT: "MY SPIRIT REJOICES"

From its beginnings, American Christianity has stressed the personal dimension of religious experience. The revivals and reform movements that have been so much a part of our Evangelical Protestant past have always emphasized some kind of personal experience of the Lord—usually of the upbeat kind, which fits in so well with our national character. During the past two decades, the Roman Catholic and Episcopal churches and some of the mainline Protestant churches have been greatly influenced by this Evangelical emphasis on personal experience of the Lord. These churches have been enriched and invigorated by personally-oriented groups and retreats such as Cursillo, Marriage Encounter, the Charismatic movements, prayer groups, various forms of Pentecostal renewal, and many other similar forms of expression. Through these renewal movements, Evangelicals, mainline Protestants, Catholics, and Episcopalians now have a common ground of religious experience. These movements have, as I have indicated, a tendency to go in the direction of spiritual narcissism. Still they are biblically based and are fostering growth in the lives of numerous Christians. These "new" emphases represent a rediscovery of an ancient strain of Spirit-filled exuberance that has deepened the life of the modern

Church immeasurably. I believe the renewal movements have helped to set a new direction for Christianity in the United States, and I hope they will eventually link up with the other significant new force in the Church: the prophetic stance with regard to peace and justice.

Though the vet' experience seems to fit more easily with the prophetic voices now challenging America than it does with the renewal movements, I believe it also has much to say to those concerned primarily with a personal encounter with Christ and with living "joyfully in the Lord." The Bible, after all, insists that light and not darkness is the ultimate spiritual reality. Jesus says to His disciples such things as "Do not be afraid" and "Peace be with you." Joy and not sorrow is the ultimate Christian state of soul. The mystical tradition, which grows out of an attempt to live closer in prayer to the God revealed in Scripture, also holds that spiritual darkness is dispelled by divine brightness. Because the Vietnam journey is akin to one stage of the classic mystical experience, it challenges Christians in the same way the mystical always does; by way of an invitation to travel beyond all boundaries and limitations of religious convention in the quest for God. Like the mystics, vets have struggled with the paradoxes that divine revelation thrusts upon us.

The first paradox has to do with religious experience. The New Testament tells us that a joyful spirit is connected with humility and lowliness rather than with power and wealth. Rejoicing in the Lord begins early in Christian history, before the birth of Jesus, in fact. Mary, a young woman whose pregnancy presented a problem to her fiancée and presumably to her neighbors, as well, hastened to visit an older cousin, also pregnant. Though her situation seemed to warrant some caution and restraint—perhaps even fear—she nonetheless greeted her cousin with the most exuberant and joyous utterance found in the New Testament: "My soul magnifies the Lord, and my spirit rejoices in God my Savior." (Luke 1:46-47) The source of her rejoicing is not that God has lifted her out of her humble position in life, rewarding her with riches and honors. Quite the contrary, she rejoices because God "has regarded the low estate of his handmaiden." Mary's exuberance of spirit continues as she gets right to the heart of what God will do for the world through the child she now bears:

> He has mercy on those who fear him in every generation. He has shown the strength of his arm, he has scattered the proud in their conceit. He has cast down the mighty from the thrones, and has lifted up the lowly. He has filled the hungry with good things and the rich he has sent away empty. (Luke 1:50-53)

Having experienced the magnificence of God's presence, Mary bursts forth in a song of praise celebrating His "mercy," which has now touched her personally. The mercy of God consists in overthrowing all proud human expectations and exalting the lowly. Mary's spirit is filled with a joy so overpowering that she must "proclaim" that God has chosen human powerlessness as the arena in which to exercise His own power. Through her yet unborn son, God has taken upon Himself human powerlessness and through it will rewrite human history as His own. The religious experience that Luke attributes to Mary is a paradigm of all subsequent Christian experience of God. It represents a complete reversal of human expectations and the conventions upon which society is based. For the Christian, this is the way God revels Himself to us; these are the grounds of his activity among us.

Paul takes up the same theme and pushes it even further. He reminds the Corinthians that God's relationship with humankind is connected to "the complete absurdity" of the cross. Through it, God has "turned the wisdom of this world into folly."

> But we preach Christ crucified—a stumbling block to the Jews, and an absurdity to the Gentiles; but to those who are called, Jews and Greeks alike, Christ the power of God and the wisdom of God. For God's folly is wiser than men, and his weakness more powerful than men. (1 Cor. 1:23-25)

Religious experience, as Christians understand it, can never be separated from the paradoxes inherent in the biblical texts. Paradox is a recognition that two contrary realities are simultaneously true. Neither reality can be denied or collapsed into the other, but each is always related to the other. Paradox calls into questions our perceptions of the world, and the temptation is always to deny or minimize the importance of one or the other reality.

Traditional American religious experience emphasizes one term on the paradox: rejoicing in God and proclaiming His greatness while minimizing the focus on the "low estate of His servant." It stresses the power and wisdom of God but ignores the notion that this is still an absurdity and a scandal because it is a power that comes by way of the cross and through human weakness. Vietnam vets, in their journey through the night of the spirit, cluster around the other reality of the Christian paradox. They know well the meaning of "low estate" but have little recent experience rejoicing in God. They relate well to folly and absurdity but have great difficulty seeing how these could be connected with the power and wisdom of God.

The consequences of these divergent emphases are clear. The journey of Vietnam vets through the night the spirit has been largely denied or not recognized as a religious reality because of the American difficulty in grasping the "folly of the cross." Nor does the notion that God scatters the proud in their conceit, casts down the mighty from their thrones, and sends the rich away empty correspond to our religious sensibilities. The Vietnam experience was largely a matter of casting down, being scattered, and sent away empty. Those who endured this experience are now themselves lowly and empty. Acquainted well with the folly and absurdity of it all, these men and women find there is no religious frame of reference through which the momentous events in their lives can be interpreted. They have had difficulty finding a spiritual home "back in the world" because the American notion of religious experience tends to deny the weakness/folly/lowly term of the paradox. When this Christian reality is collapsed into the greatness/power/rejoicing dimension as representing the only aspect of God's presence among us, a grave distortion takes place.

This historical distortion is evident in our form of civil religion, which passes itself off as Christianity. It is evident also in our continuing inability to connect our personal quest for God with a commitment to working for peace in the world and securing justice for the hungry and lowly. Distortion is the only word which can describe the popularity of the TV religious hucksters hustling "big bucks" for Jesus and the connection so many people make between religious faith and material success. The distortion becomes most grotesque when a people who claim to rejoice in the Lord arm to fight for His purposes. The Song of Mary and the teaching of Paul lose their meaning in such a context.

The renewal movements now enlivening the Church can correct the distortion by reclaiming the New Testament vision and by affirming once again that we can truly rejoice in the Lord and proclaim His greatness only if we embrace the "Folly" of the cross and recognize anew His presence in the powerless. Vietnam vets in their pilgrimage through the night present a newly exuberant Church with an opportunity to regain its grasp on the full range of the Christian paradox.

The contrary is also true. A religious distortion exists

among Vietnam vets who have only just begun to recognize the religious meaning of their journey in darkness. Absurdity, folly, low estate, and powerlessness of themselves can be destructive conditions. Unredeemed by God and untouched by grace, they often lead to rage, nihilism, or dangerous apathy. The cross is indeed absurd unless it is connected with the hope of resurrection. The haunting sense of God's absence/presence, which lingers in the consciousness of so many vets, is an invitation to learn what God can do among those of low estate who are now empty and powerless, people for whom the conventional terms of life no longer have meaning. For the dark night of the soul to be a pilgrimage, a prelude rather than an endless journey, one must be receptive to the power of God, which leads to rejoicing. By embracing the Church, which has learned to "sing a new song unto the Lord, vets may regain their hold on that dimension of the paradox that has eluded them.

Personal religious experience, no matter how significant it may be, is not the final reality of the Christian faith: God is. Our own experience—whether it is of the exuberant or the wintry kind—only leads us to God who has revealed Himself to the world and to us. In our own personal search for the signature of God etched upon the world, we confront another paradox: creation itself.

In the second creation story in the Book of Genesis (Gen. 2:4-3:24), we find that God creates humankind in the garden of His favor. Essential to humanity is the ability to make free choices—to eat of the fruit from the tree of knowledge of good and evil. The first—and perennial—use of human freedom is the choice of evil: sin. The paradox endures for all time. The all-powerful Creator gives to His own creation the power to disobey, to reject him and to destroy each other. This is a power that is never rescinded. Expulsion from the garden and the other consequences of sin are clearly drawn in the story—and in human history. Almost hidden within the story, however, is a further paradox, the obscure promise of redemption (the "off-spring" who will strike at the head of the serpent; verse 15).

The question asked of God in anger by the ex-Marine in Chapter 1 takes on a different hue within the context of the creation paradox. In Vietnam we were simply living out in vivid terms the consequences of human freedom. We were doing it to ourselves. This is the story of all the wars and genocides throughout history. To demand a coercive presence of God restricting our freedom to sin, no matter how horrendously evil the sin might be, is to misunderstand the creation story. We must search instead for the meaning of that obscure promise of redemption. The unfolding history in the Hebrew and Christian Scriptures is God's continuing revelation of what that promise means. A personal journey out of the night is never accomplished by a demand for any kind of coercion, even God's, but rather a pilgrimage freely undertaken in search of redemption.

The New Testament story reveals a final paradox. God, who is so far above us, so beyond our powers of intellect and imagination, finally bridged the distance between Himself and us in a marvelous way: He became physical with us. He slipped quietly, unobtrusively, into our history and our personal lives as an infant born in obscurity. Now we could know Him and grasp Him in the only way we can—physically.

One term of the paradox, God's transcendent power, becomes progressively more incomprehensible and beyond imagination as we learn more about the reality that surrounds us. We now understand that the universe, His creation, consists of billions of galaxies with more than two hundred billion stars separated by aeons of time and vast distances. We are able to comprehend God only because He surrendered His own power to come among us. In His own lowliness, we recognize Him and respond to Him.

The images of Jesus, a man of low estate, flesh out the promise and the hope hidden in the creation story. The young carpenter turned preacher, announcing that the kingdom of God had arrived and was to be filled with the poor, the hungry, and the outcast, provides an image of immense power in a world of refugees and the destitute. The victim of a brutal and unjust execution, forgiving his murderers moments before death, is an image that reaches through twenty centuries to a world of countless wars and a monstrous arms race. Images of an empty tomb and a risen Lord remind us that God is one who overturns the world's gulag. The final New Testament image is one of power. The obscure infant and helpless victim becomes the final judge of all and Lord of history who demands an accounting on behalf of the hungry, thirsty, naked, sick, and imprisoned.

No Christian can evade the biblical paradoxes. Those who wander in the desert of the soul and those who rejoice in the Lord are alike invited to join with Christ in his own journey out of the night. The very earliest Christians understood the journey well and composed a hymn about it. Paul discovered the hymn and incorporated it into one of his letters.

> Your attitude must be that of Christ:
> Though he was in the form of God,
>> he did not deem equality with God
>> something to be grasped at.
> Rather, he emptied himself
>> and took the form of a slave,
>> Being born in the likeness of men.
> He was known to be of human estate,
>> and it was thus that he humbled himself,
>> Obediently accepting even death,
>> death on a cross!
> Because of this,
>> God highly exalted him
>> and bestowed on him the name.
>> above every other name,

So that at Jesus' name
>> every knee must bend
>> in the heavens, on the earth,
>> and under the earth,
>> and every tongue proclaim
>> to the glory of God the Father:
>>> Jesus Christ is Lord. (Phil. 2:5-11)

The journey is not an easy one. No one knew this better than Paul, who struggled throughout life with his own weakness. He implored God to remove his personal "sting of the flesh," but he finally understood that God's grace was sufficient and that strength was made perfect in weakness. He came at last to peace within himself: "God's own peace which is beyond all understanding." (Phil. 4:7)

Perhaps the journey out of the night ends with a peace that indeed goes beyond any understanding. If so, I suspect it includes a contagious impulse to extend peace to others. Perhaps it is embodied in a desire to "hug a Russian"—or a vet, a war protester, a Vietnamese, a Moslem, an atheist, a "secular humanist," or whoever one's current enemies happen to be. Perhaps it is a greeting engraved on the heart and extended to all:

> May he who is the Lord of peace give you continued peace in every possible way. The Lord be with you all. (2 Thess. 3:16)

APPENDIX:
LITURGY OF RECONCILIATION

LITURGY OF RECONCILIATION Feb. 27, 1985
La Casa de Maria, Santa Barbara
Ten Years After Vietnam: A Time For Healing

Song

Bless the Lord who forgives all our sins. *(priest)*
His mercy endures forever. *(all)*
Almighty God, to you all hearts are open, all desires known, and from you no secrets are hid: Cleanse the thoughts of our hearts by the inspiration of your Holy Spirit, that we may perfectly love you and worthily magnify your holy Name; through Christ our Lord. Amen.
Lord have mercy. Christ have mercy. Lord have mercy.
Prayer *(all)*
Lord, you have delivered us from the scourge of war. May we who have been scarred by war be reconciled to each other, to our enemies, and to you. May we become peacemakers in all that we do. May we be always agents and instruments of your peace. Grant to those who are as yet untouched by war the great gift of continued freedom from the terrible agonies of armed

conflict. We ask this through Jesus Christ, your Son, our Lord. Amen.

1st Reading *Isa.* 2:2-5
Song
2nd Reading 1 *John* 3:11-16
Song
Gospel *Matt.* 5:38-48
Reflections
Prayers of the People
1. *Intercessions*
2. *Thanksgiving*
3. *Praise*

Confession of Sin
1. *Humble yourself...*
2. *Personal reflection*
3. *Confession (all)*

Most merciful God, we confess that we have sinned against you in thought, word, and deed, by what we have done, and by what we have left undone. We have not loved you with our whole heart; we have not loved our neighbors as ourselves. We are truly sorry and we humbly repent. We are sorry especially for our sins of violence and hatred. For the sake of your son Jesus Christ, have mercy on us and forgive us; that we may delight in your will and walk in your ways, to the glory of your Name. Amen.

4. *Absolution (priest)*

May the God of peace grant you forgiveness of all your sins especially those of hatred, violence, and the harboring of evil. As a minister of the Gospel of Jesus Christ, I proclaim to you the forgiveness of your sins and the mercy of God.

The Peace

Song

The Great Thanksgiving (based on *Isa.* 2:2-5, 1 *John* 3:11-16, *Matt.* 5:38-48, and The Book of Common Prayer)

The Lord be with you.

And also with you.

Lift up your hearts.

We lift them to the Lord.

Let us give thanks to the Lord our God.

It is right to give him thanks and praise.

God of all power, Ruler of the universe, you are worthy of glory and praise. For you have revealed your will that all peoples without number should come to your holy mountain in peace to learn your ways and walk in your paths. You have called us to hammer our swords into ploughshares and our spears into sickles. You have revealed your will that nation should not lift sword against nation.

Again and again you have called us to live in peace. Yet we have sinned against you, refusing to love, committing the sin of Cain. But you have loved us, sending to us the prophets and sages, revealing your righteous law. Finally, in the fullness of time you sent your only Son, born of a woman, to open for us the way of freedom and peace.

Therefore, we praise you, joining the angels and saints in proclaiming your glory as we sing.

    Holy, holy, holy Lord, God of power and
        might, heaven
    and earth are full of your glory.
    Hosanna in the highest.
    Blessed is he who comes in the name of the
        Lord.
    Hosanna in the highest.

And so, Father, we who have been redeemed by him, and made a new people by water and the Spirit are gathered together in peace. We stand before you today, mindful that your Son has commanded us to love our enemies and pray for those who persecute us. Conscious of our sin, we ask to be reconciled to you and to each other through your Son. We offer to you these gifts of bread and wine. Sanctify them by your Holy Spirit to be the Body and Blood of Jesus Christ our Lord.

On the night he was betrayed, he took bread, said the blessing, broke the bread, and gave it to his friends, and said: "Take, eat: This is my Body, which is given for you. Do this for the remembrance of me."

After supper, he took the cup of wine, gave thanks, and said: "Drink this, all of you. This is my Blood of the new Covenant, which is shed for you and for many for the forgiveness of sins. Whenever you drink it, do this for the remembrance of me."

Therefore we proclaim the Mystery of Faith:

Christ has died. (all)

Christ has risen.

Christ will come again.

Lord, God of peace, open our minds and hearts to the gracious gift of your son, our Lord. Through the power of his death may we die to our own sinful selves and come alive again in the newness of life and in the peace which you have given to us through him. Let the grace of this Holy Communion make us one body, one spirit in Christ, that we may be to the world the messengers and bearers of his peace.

Through Him and with Him and in Him, in the Unity of the Holy Spirit all honor and glory is yours, Almighty Father, now and forever. AMEN.

The Lord's Prayer
The Breaking of Bread
Christ our Passover is sacrificed for us.

Therefore let us keep the feast.

Communion

Song

Postcommunion prayer (all)

Lord, you have graciously accepted us as living members of your Son our Savior Jesus Christ and you have fed us with spiritual food in the Sacrament of his Body and Blood. Send us now into the world in peace and grant us strength and courage to love and serve you with gladness and singleness of heart through Christ our Lord. AMEN.

Blessing

Dismissal

Song

NOTES

CHAPTER ONE

1. Unpublished account of veteran's experience.
2. *Ibid.*
3. Philip Caputo, *A Rumor of War,* p.321.
4. Ron Kovic, *Born on the Fourth of July,* p.193.
5. Mark Baker, *Nam,* pp.135-36.
6. Interview in Al Santoli, *Everything We Had,* p.208.
7. *Ibid.,* p.63.
8. Loren Baritz, *Backfire,* pp.24-25.
9. Interview in Santoli, *Everything We Had,* p. 208.
4. Ibid., p.205.
11. *Ibid., pp.195-96.*
12. Lynda Van Devanter with Christopher Morgan, *Home Before Morning,* p.166.
13. *Ibid.,* p.106.

CHAPTER TWO

14. Baker, *Nam,* p.262.
15. *Ibid.,* p.263.
16. Van Devanter, *Home Before Morning,* p.247.
17. *Ibid.,* p.248.
18. Baker, *Nam,* p.267.
19. Myra Macpherson, *Long Time Passing: Vietnam and the Haunted Generation,* p.82.
20. *Ibid.,* p. 82.
21. *Ibid.,* p.83.
22. *Ibid.,* p.83.

CHAPTER THREE

23. Gloria Emerson, *Winners and Losers,* p. 331.
24. Robert Jay Lifton, "Advocacy and Corruption in the Healing Profession" in Charles R. Figley (ed.), *Stress Disorders Among Vietnam Veterans,* p.212.
25. *Ibid.*
26. W. Taylor Stevenson, "The Experience of Defilement: A Response to John wheeler," *Anglican Theological Review,* vol. LXIV, no. 1, p.25.

CHAPTER FOUR

27. American Psychiatric Association, *Diagnostic and Statistical Manual of Mental Disorders,* 3rd. ed. *(DSM III),* and *DAV,* vol.22, no.1, list "post Vietnam" symptoms.
28. Bruce Goderez, M.D., "The Many Faces of Posttraumatic Stress Disorder" *Vet Center Voice,* vol.7, no.1, p.7.
29. *Ibid.,* p.8.
30. *DSM III,* pp.236-39 lists category 309.81 "post-traumatic stress disorder."
31. Clark Smith, "The Soldier-Cynics: Veterans Still Caught in the War," *Southeast Asia Chronicle,* no.85, p.12.
32. *Ibid.,* p.12.
33. Peter Marin, "Living in Moral Pain," *Psychology* Today, vol. 15, no.11.
34. *Ibid.,* p.72.
35. *Ibid.,* p.74.
36. Michael Waizer, Just *and Unjust Wars: A Moral Argument with Historical Illustrations,* pp.195-96.
37. *Ibid.,* p.311.
38. Marin, "Living in Moral Pain," p.79.
39. *Ibid.*
40. Steve Mason, *Johnny's Song,* p.97.

41. *Ibid.,* p.98.
42. Marin, "Living in Moral Pain," p.80.
43. In his book *Backfire,* Loren Barit: shows the extent to which bureaucratic procedures and management theory have become entrenched in the military establishment.

CHAPTER FIVE

44. Caputo, *A Rumor of War,* pp. xvii-xviii.
45. *Ibid.,* pp. xvii-xviii.
46. Peter Goldman and Tony Fuller, *Charlie Company: What* Vietnam' *Did To Us,* p.208.
47. *Ibid.,* p.213.
48. *Ibid.,* p.213.
49. Ibid., pp. 156-57.
50. *Ibid.,* pp. 284-85.
51. Interview reported in Jeffrey C. Dube, "What Happened to Our Master?" p.11. The loss of religious faith among Vietnam veterans as a consequence of their military service has also been studied by Douglas L. Anderson, "The Vietnam Combat Veteran: His Experience, His Faith and Faith Development."
52. Michael Norman, "Chaplains are Torn Between Allegiance to God and Army," *Denver Post,* August 15, 1982.
53. Interview in Dube, "What Happened to Our Master?," p.9.
54. *Ibid.*
55. Michael Herr, *Dispatches,* pp.46-47.
56. Lifton, "Advocacy and Corruption in the Healing Profession," pp.218-20.
57. Kovic, *Born on the Fourth of July,* p. 185.
58. Emerson, *Winners and Losers, p.50.*
59. John Winthrop's sermon as found in Russell Riche and Donald Jones, *American Civil Religion,* p.267.
60. *Ibid.*

61. Robert N. Bellab, with Richard Madden, William M. Sullivan, Ann Seidler, Steve M. Tiptoe, *Habits of the Heart,* p. 29.
62. The term "nation with the soul of a church" was coined by G.K. Chesterton. The term is also used by Sydney E. Mead as a title: Chesterton. The term is also used by Sydney E. Mead as a title:"The Nation with the Soul of a Church," first published in *Church History,* vol.36, no.3, and reprinted in Riche, *American Civil Religion.*
63. Herbert Richardson, "Civil Religion in Theological Perspective," in Riche,   *American Civil Religion,* p. 164.
64. Urban T. Holmes, *Turning to Christ,* p.136.
65. Walter Capps began teaching a dass on the Vietnam war at the University of California, Santa Barbara in 1977. The class has become immensely popular with students, now drawing over 900 students each time it is taught. Capps is also the author of *The Unfinished War: Vietnam and the American Conscience.*
66. Galen Mayer, "The Vietnam War and Joseph Conrad's *Heart of Darkness,*" *Pro Rege,*   vol. Xl, no.4, pp.8-9.
67. *Ibid.,* p.l0.
68. *Ibid.,* p. 12.
69. Santiago Sia, "Reflections on Job's Question," *Spirituality Today,* vol.37, no.3, p.239.

CHAPTER SIX

70. John L. McKenzie, S.J., *Dictionary of the Bible,* p.598.
71. *Ibid.,* p.599.
72. The distinction between biblical religion and mythology using the Romulus and Remus story was made by the French scholar, Rene Girard, in a lecture given at the University of California, San Diego, in 1985.
73. John Ferguson, "A Man of sorrows, Familiar with

Suffering," an interview in *The* Olympia *Churchmen,* July/August 1985, p.6.

74. Timothy Calhoun Sims, "Gulag and Kyrie," *LCA Partners,* vol. v, no.3, p.10.

75. *Ibid.*

76. *Ibid.*

77. *Ibid.*

78. *Ibid.*

79. Ferguson, "A Man of Sorrow, Familiar With Suffering," p.6.

80. *Ibid.*

81. Kenneth Leech, *True Prayer,* p.22.

82. *Ibid.,* p.105-6.

83. Bellab, et al., *Habits of the Heart,* p.127.

84. *Ibid.,* p.232.

CHAPTER SEVEN

85. Martin E. Marty, *A Cry* of *Absence,* pp.2-3.

86. Anonymous author, ed. William Johnston, *The Cloud of Un-knowing,* pp.48-49.

87. Ralph A. Keifer, "A Spirituality of Mystery," *Spirituality Today,* vol.33, no.2, p.100.

88. *Ibid., p.105.*

89 *Ibid.*, p. 107.

90. Anonymous author, *The Cloud of Unknowing, p.50.*

91. *Ibid.,* pp.53-54.

BIBLIOGRAPHY

American Psychiatric Association. *Diagnostic and Statistical Manual of Mental Disorder*. 3rd. ed. Washington, D.C.: American Psychiatric Association, 1980.

Anderson, Douglas L. "The Vietnam Combat Veteran: His Experience, His Faith and Faith Development." Master's thesis, North American Baptist Seminary, Sioux Falls, South Dakota, 1985.

Anonymous. *The Cloud of Unknowing*. Edited by William Johnston. Garden City, N.Y.: Image Books, 1973.
This fourteenth century book is a classic on the Christian mystical experience. The unknown author speaks to our contemporary world of knowing God in the face of his apparent absence in a "cloud of unknowing." It is a book of tremendous power.

Baker, Mark. *Nam*. New York: William Morrow, 1980; reprinted, New York: Berkley Books, 1981.

Hundreds of individual stories of Vietnam vets. An excellent book for acquiring a perspective on the diversity of the vets' experiences.

Baritz, Loren. *Backfire: A History of How American Culture Led Us into Vietnam and Made Us Fight the Way We Did*. New York: William Morrow, *1985;* reprint edition, New York: Ballantine Books, 1986.

The author probes the assumptions of American culture which

led us into Vietnam. His analysis is penetrating, his arguments convincing. An excellent book.

Bellab, Robert N.; with Madden, Richard; Sullivan, William M.; Swindler, Ann; Tipton, Steven. *Habits of the Heart*. Berkeley: University of California Press, 1985; reprint edition, New York: Harper & Row, 1986.
The authors pursue the questions raised by Alexis de Tocqueville in his 1830s analysis of American culture. A thorough and profound study of how Americans of the 1980s think, feel, and live. The book's fundamental question is how do we preserve or create a morally coherent life?

The Book of Common Prayer. Kingsport, Tennessee: Kingsport Press, 1977.
Official Prayer Book of the Episcopal Church.

Capps, Walter. *The Unfinished War: Vietnam and the American Conscience*. Boston: Beacon Press, 1982.
The author uses historical and analytic tools to relate his extensive first-hand knowledge of Vietnam vets and make the case that Vietnam is an unfinished war in the American conscience. As such, he believes, the war presents a real danger that history will repeat itself as our political and religious leaders advocate a return to outmoded ideals.

Caputo, Philip. *A Rumor of War*. New York: Holt, Rinehart, and Winston, 1977; reprint edition, New York: Ballantine Books, 1978.
One of the great books to come out of the Vietnam war, written by a Marine Corps veteran.

"Delayed Stress Reaction." *DAV*, vol. 22, no. 1 (January 1980), Cold Spring, Kentucky.

Official publication of Disabled American Veterans.

Dube, Jeffrey C. "What Happened to Our Master?" Master's thesis, Bangor Theological Seminary, Bangor, Maine, *1985*.

Emerson, Gloria. *Winners and Losers*. New York: Random House, Inc., 1972.
An early and serious look at the Vietnam war and its veterans. It remains a classic.

Ferguson, John. "A Man of Sorrows, Familiar with Suffering." Interview. *The Olympia Churchman* (July/August 1985).

Goderez, Bruce M.D. "The Many Faces of Posttraumatic Stress Disorder." *Vet Center Voice,* vol. 7, no. 1 January 1986).
A Fargo publication of the Readjustment Counseling Service, Veterans Administration.

Goldman, Peter, and Fuller, Tony. *Charlie Company: What Vietnam Did To Us*. New York: William Morrow, 1982; reprint edition, New York: Ballantine Books, 1983.
A close look at a single unit which went through some heavy fighting. It follows the veterans as they return and pick up their lives "back in the world."

Herr, Michael. *Dispatches*. New York: Alfred A. Knopf, Inc., 1968; reprint edition, New York: Avon Books, 1978.
The author, a journalist, captures the flavor of what it was really like in Vietnam. The madness of the place can be relived in the pages of this book. Must reading for anyone who wasn't there.

Holmes, Urban T. *Turning to Christ*. New York: The Seabury Press, 1981.

Karnow, Stanley. *Vietnam: A History*. New York: The Viking Press, 1983; reprint edition, London: Penguin Books, 1984. An exhaustive history of the Vietnam war.

Kifer, Ralph A. "A Spirituality of Mystery." *Spirituality Today*, vol. 33, no. 2 (June 1981). A publication of the Chicago Dominicans, Province of St. Albert the Great.

Kovic, Ron. *Born on the Fourth of July*. New York: McGraw Hill, 1976; reprint edition, New York: Pocket Books, 1984. One of the first—and still one of the best—autobiographies by a veteran.

Kushner, Harold S. *When Bad Things Happen to Good People*. New York: Shocken Books, 1981; reprint edition, New York: Avon Books, 1982.

Leech, Kenneth. *True Prayer*. San Francisco: Harper and Row, 1980.

Lifton, Robert Jay. "Advocacy and Corruption in the Healing Profession." *In Stress Disorders Among Vietnam Veterans*, edited by Charles R. Figley. New York: Brunner/Mazel, 1978.

Macpherson, Myra. *Long Time Passing*. Garden City, N.Y.: Doubleday & Company, Inc., 1984. An exhaustive study of the Vietnam generation. The author listens to veterans, anti-war protesters, and others of that generation. Her analysis is excellent.

Marin, Peter. *"Living in Moral Pain."* Psychology Today, vol. 15, no. 11 (November 1981).

This article has been used widely by veteran counselors. Marin's insights are profound.

Marty, Martin E. *A Cry of Absence*. San Francisco: Harper and Row, 1983.
A profound, moving, and easy-to-read treatment of God's apparent absence *from* contemporary life. For anyone who has experienced the "winter of the spirit."

Mason, Steve. *Johnny's Song*. New York: Bantam Books, 1986.
The poet laureate of the Vietnam Veterans of America, Mason writes poetry of incredible power. He reaches to the heart of the vets' experiences as only a poet can.

McKenzie, John L., S.J. *Dictionary of the Bible*. New York: The Macmillan Company, 1965.

Meyer, Galen. "The Vietnam War and Joseph Conrad's *Heart of Darkness*." *Pro Rege*, vol. Xl, no. 4 (June 1983).
A publication of Dordt College, Sioux City, Iowa.

Norman, Michael. "Chaplains Are Torn Between Allegiance to God and Army." *The Denver Post*, August 15, 1982.

Richey, Russell, and Jones, Donald G. *American Civil Religion*. New York: Harper and Row, 1974.

Santoli, AL. *Everything We Had*. New York: Random House, 1980; reprint edition, New York: Ballantine Books, 1981.
A fine book. It consists of thirty-three oral histories of the war by veterans.

Sia, Santiago. "Reflections on Job's Question." *Spirituality*

Today, vol. 37, no. 3 (Fall 1985).
A publication of the Chicago Dominicans, Province of St. Albert the Great.

Sims, Timothy Calhoun. "Gulag and Kyrie," *LCA Partners*, vol. V, no. 3 June 1983).
A publication of Lutheran Church in America, Philadelphia.

Smith, Clark. "The Soldier-Cynics: Veterans Still Caught in a War." *Southeast Asia Chronicle*, no. 85 (August 1982).
A publication of the Berkeley Southeast Asia Resource Center.

Stevenson, W. Taylor. "The Experience of Defilement: A Response to John Wheeler." *Anglican Theological Review*, vol. LXIV, no. 1 January 1982).
A publication of the Seabury Western Theological Seminary, Chicago.

Van Devanter, Lynda, with Morgan, Christopher. *Home Before Morning*. New York: Beaufort Books, 1982; reprint edition, New York, Warner Books, 1983.
A very moving autobiography: the experiences of a nurse in Vietnam.

Walker, Michael. *Just and Unjust Wars: A Moral Argument with Historical Illustrations*. New York: Basic Books, Inc., 1977.
An excellent treatment of the moral issues connected with war. Extensive use of historical cases to illustrate arguments.

Made in the USA
Lexington, KY
09 September 2015